SIGNS OF CATECHESIS

SIGNS OF CATECHESIS

*An Overview of the
National Catechetical Directory*

by

Anne Marie Mongoven, O.P.

PAULIST PRESS
New York/Ramsey/Toronto

Library of Congress
Catalog Card Number: 78-58964

ISBN: 0-8091-2152-2

Published by Paulist Press
Editorial Office: 1865 Broadway, New York, N.Y. 10023
Business Office: 545 Island Road, Ramsey, N.J. 07446

Printed and bound in the
United States of America

Contents

Contents

*To my Mother and Father,
my first and best catechists.*

Acknowledgments

Writing the directory was a task in which thousands of persons participated. Many of their insights into the nature and purpose of catechesis were incorporated into the directory and consequently into this overview of it. However, as a close participant in the directory's development, I need especially to acknowledge the insights gained from the members of the directory committee and from Monsignor Wilfrid Paradis and Sr. Mariella Frye, the directors of its development. Grateful acknowledgment is also made to Rita Claire Dorner, O.P. and Maureen Gallagher whose encouragement and useful criticism were of invaluable assistance to me.

Foreword

There is no similarity between catechetics and wine-making except that both arts are known to have vintage years. For catechetics 1977 was such a year when circumstances coincided to produce a remarkable yield. Never before in the history of the Church had the hierarchy given so much concentrated attention to this facet of the ministry of the word.

In October bishops from around the world gathered in Synod in Rome to discuss "Catechesis in Our Time." It turned out to be, according to one observer, "the most convincing sign of the Church's renewal since Vatican II." It opened up new and, for many, undreamed of horizons.

A month later the bishops of the United States gathered in Washington for their annual meeting. The main item on the agenda was the national catechetical directory. It was an impressive sight to see virtually all the Catholic prelates in the country—nearly 300 strong—work their way through the document line by line, hour after hour. At the end, they approved almost unanimously *Sharing the Light of Faith*, their title for the directory. Their vote capped a project that had been six years in the making.

When the project of a catechetical directory was

first broached at the bishops' meeting in 1971, no one anticipated the work it would entail. While many felt the need for some authoritative guidelines to bring focus and direction to the many and varied educational ministries in the Church, few grasped the scope of the undertaking. A short time later the bishops issued *Basic Teachings for Catholic Religious Education* and *To Teach as Jesus Did*, a pastoral letter on Catholic education. It was like pouring new wine into old wineskins for these documents needed to be integrated into the general pattern of renewal framed by Vatican II. The General Catechetical Directory mandated by the council had outlined basic principles governing the nature and objectives of catechesis. It was a first step but these general guidelines had to be spelled out more specifically for the American scene.

Sharing the Light of Faith is a comprehensive survey of the aims and goals, the contents and context, the means and organization of catechesis in the United States. Nothing like it had ever been attempted before. In a book of modest size it presents a remarkable syllabus of the outstanding elements of Christian faith, an introduction to sacramental theology, a primer in educational theory and developmental psychology, and a survey of the pastoral ministries in the U.S. as well as a summary statement of catechetical guidelines. Unfortunately, its success contains the potential seeds for its own undoing. In bringing these disparate elements together in one volume, *Sharing the Light of Faith* is in danger of loosing its readers in the foliage of detail.

Despite the efforts of the authors and editors to keep it simple, ordinary readers are likely to find

themselves asking with the Ethiopian eunuch, "How
can I understand unless someone will give me a
clue?" (Acts, 8:31). Few are better suited to explaining the directory than Anne Marie Mongoven, O.P.
Having done catechesis at every level from pre-school
through adult education programs, and having
taught catechetics in graduate programs, she can
anticipate the kinds of questions people will ask
about the directory. Because of her position on the
working committee which prepared the text of the
directory, she knows where to find the clues that
unlock its meaning.

Signs of Catechesis is in fact a digest of the contents of the national directory. By summarizing the
contents under headings of four signs—biblical, ecclesial, liturgical, and natural—she offers an organi-
zational framework which makes it easy to see the
way the parts of *Sharing the Light of Faith* relate to
each other. Knowing the sources it drew on and the
emphasis it intends, Sister Mongoven is able to cut
away unnecessary detail which was unavoidable in
the original document. Her system of cross-
references makes it easy to find one's way through
the pages of the directory without getting lost in the
underbrush of repetition.

As a special consultant to the staff, I was able to
observe Sister Mongoven emerge as one of the leaders
of the working committee. All her colleagues, even
those who did not always see eye to eye with her,
acknowledge that she exercised a dominant influence
on shaping the vision and scope of the directory sometimes by her forcefully argued recommendations and
at other times by drafting sections of it herself. Her
contribution to the directory continues here in the

pages of the *Signs of Catechesis*. She shows that *Sharing the Light of Faith* is another convincing sign of the Church's continuing renewal, opening for many undreamed horizons in catechesis.

Berard L. Marthaler, OFMConv.
Department of Religion and Religious Education
The Catholic University of America

Introduction

How the Directory Came To Be

In December 1973, the first consultation on the proposed national catechetical directory began. Four years later, in November 1977, the bishops of this country approved such a directory. It was recently published under the title *Sharing the Light of Faith*.

"What is a directory?" is a question that was asked frequently during the consultation process. Indeed, recommendations for the directory indicated that some people thought of it as a catechism, a compendium of the doctrines of the Church.

A directory is a relatively new form of writing in the Church. It is not a catechism. It is a pastoral writing which sets goals for catechesis, suggests means for achieving these goals, and furnishes guidelines for implementing the catechetical ministry. National directories differ from the *General Catechetical Directory* in that they apply the principles of the GCD to concrete cultural circumstances. They promote and coordinate the catechetical ministry in a particular nation (GCD 17).

The catechetical directory for the Church in the United States is a lengthy document. It treats of many different issues, including among them such

varied topics as cultural and religious characteristics affecting catechesis in this country,
catechesis and human development, a brief overview
of Catholic social teaching, and the principal elements of the Christian message. The wide range and
diversity of its concerns indicate that there is in the
United States a new understanding of the nature,
goals, and scope of the catechetical ministry.

    Sharing the Light of Faith reflects in many ways
the Roman Catholic Church in the United States. A
nation of over 200 million people of different racial,
ethnic, and cultural backgrounds, with added differ-
ences due to geographic regional influence, educational background, and age, cannot be neatly described in a short, tidy package. The directory reflects the pluralistic views and styles of life of our
people.

    It is also a document that reflects the United
States in the way that it was written. *Sharing the
Light of Faith* is an official document of the National
Conference of Catholic Bishops. It was approved by
the bishops by a vote of 216 to 12 at their annual
meeting in Washington in November, 1977. In December, 1977, it was submitted to the Sacred Congregation for the Clergy for review and approval.
This approval was granted October 30, 1978.

    This document is unique in the history of the
Church in the United States because of the way in
which it was written. This process, mandated by the
bishops, included the formation of a National
Catechetical Directory Committee, which was given
decision-making authority in all aspects of the development of the document, and a decision to publish
all drafts of the proposed directory for consultation.

The entire Church in the United States was invited to participate in its formation.

The National Catechetical Directory Committee was composed of four bishops, two laywomen, one layman, two sisters, one brother, one religious priest, and one diocesan priest. These persons represented a variety of cultural backgrounds and catechetical experiences. They had differing competencies and interests. They represented insofar as possible what Monsignor Wilfrid Paradis and Sister Mariella Frye, directors of the project, called a "microcosm" of the Catholic Church in the United States.

As a member of this committee, I would like to state publicly that we were given complete freedom in our work. We studied, discussed, debated, argued, prayed, and celebrated together. When difficulties arose, we worked through them. We grew in our understanding of the nature, purpose, and goals of catechesis. We achieved a remarkable consensus, though not always unanimity, in our decisions. It was a privilege to work with such dedicated Christians, each of whom contributed much of himself or herself to this task. The other members of the committee were Archbishop John F. Whealon, Archbishop William D. Borders, Bishop Mark Hurley, Bishop Kenneth J. Povish, Miss Mary Baylouny, Sister Celia Ann Cavazos, Mr. Thomas Lawler, Rev. James Lyke, Mrs. Gerard (Joan) O'Keefe, Brother Cosmas Rubencamp, and Rev. William A. Wassmuth.

Two theologians, Rev. Berard Marthaler and Rev. Alfred McBride attended our meetings and acted as consultants to the committee. When we realized we needed special help in regard to Eastern Catholic Churches' perspectives, Msgr. Seeley Beggiani and Rev. John Zeyack were appointed as consultants.

The National Directory Committee also worked with a committee of bishops called the Bishops' Committee of Policy and Review. The eight bishops on this committee set general policy for the directory and periodically reviewed the work of the directory committee.

The consultation process involved three stages. Before a single sentence of the directory was written, a proposed topical outline was drawn up and published. Invitations to comment on the outline and to make recommendations or suggestions for the proposed directory were sent to every diocese in the country and to every national society or agency in the United States even remotely concerned with religious education. Scholars in various sacred and human sciences were also invited to participate in the consultation. Approximately 32,000 individuals responded with recommendations.

These recommendations were analyzed and studied. A new outline was formulated, and the first draft was written. This draft was published in tabloid form in December 1974. Over 650,000 copies were circulated. Because of the importance of the Spanish-speaking communities in the Church in the United States, the draft was also published in Spanish. Approximately 80,000 recommendations from parents, cathechists, clergy, religious, professional religious educators, scholars from various disciplines, and other adult members of the church were received.

These recommendations were again carefully studied, discussed and debated by the NCD committee. Then recommendations for the revised draft were made. A careful study of the revised draft will show that some major changes were made. These changes were directly related to the criticisms, information, and specific recommendations that came from the consultation process. Of course, contradictory recommendations were received. The NCD committee exercised its own judgment in responding to these contradictions.

Consultation on the second or revised draft was carried on between January 1, and March 31, 1977. This third consultation differed from the first two in that the results of the consultation were analyzed in each individual diocese. Each diocese prepared a report for the national office. This report presented the recommendations from the diocese and any recommendations the bishop of the diocese wished to make. During this third consultation, the N.C.D. Office continued to consult directly with scholars and national organizations.

The NCD committee met in July, 1977, to prepare its final revision of the document. This revision was sent to the Bishops' Committee of Policy and Review for their approval. This committee made minor revisions and then sent the prepared text to each bishop for his recommendations. Once this revision was completed by the NCD committee, its work was finished. Completion of the directory became the work of the bishops themselves.

Sharing the Light of Faith is an official document of the National Conference of Catholic Bishops. But because of the extensive process of consultation, the directory is, in fact, a document that reflects not only the bishops, but also much of the Roman Catholic community in the United States.

It is a consensus document representing a position that is neither avant-garde nor static. It reflects the position of the Church as to the nature and goals of catechesis. It ratifies the catechetical renewal of the past quarter-century.

The directory ratifies renewal in many ways. It officially accepts growth in faith for both individuals and communities as the goal of catechesis. The priority to be given to the catechesis of adults is a constant refrain that permeates the entire document. A model of catechesis that is concerned with the totality of the lives of individuals and communities replaces the instructional or schooling model of catechesis. Social justice is acknowledged as a constitutive element in all catechesis.

The directory consists of eleven chapters. Each chapter centers on a particular catechetical issue but some topics are, of necessity, treated in several chapters. For example, guidelines for the catechesis of adults are found in almost every chapter of *Sharing the Light of Faith*. Because there is so much overlapping of topics within the directory, an analysis of the directory on a chapter by chapter basis does not bring together the fullness with which the directory treats each topic.

Signs of Catechesis represents an attempt to unify the main points of the directory. Whenever the directory treats of a catechetical issue in several chapters we have tried to bring together the principal points of its treatment. The directory's own framework of unity, that is, the four signs of catechesis, are the framework on which this book has been designed. Chapters and articles in the directory which refer to the catechetical signs have been listed on charts which appear in this book.

Sharing the Light of Faith is a lengthy document. One of the more vexing problems the writers faced was the question of how lengthy the document should be. At one point the directory committee attempted to shorten the directory to one half the size of the first draft. Later it decided that the document should be as short as possible without sacrificing content. Key concepts and issues were retained but they were not always fully developed. At the time of the final voting on the document over 40 typewritten pages were added by the bishops.

The directory has a preface and eleven chapters. The preface includes background information on the directory itself as well as a brief overview of catechetical developments in this century. Chapter one treats of some cultural and religious characteristics which affect catechesis in the United States. In chapter two the nature, goals, and forms of catechesis are considered. This chapter presents the framework around which the rest of the directory is built. Revelation and faith as related to catechesis are discussed in chapter three. The ecclesial signs, Church and message are treated in chapters four and five respectively. Chapter six examines catechesis and the liturgical signs. Catechesis for social ministry or service, the third ecclesial sign, is presented in chapter seven. Chapter eight discusses faith and human development, or the natural signs. The role of the catechist is considered in chapter nine. Chapters ten and eleven discuss organization for catechesis and catechetical resources.

Signs of Catechesis is a guide to reading *Sharing the Light of Faith*. It contains a summary as well as some commentary on the document. Reading this book is not meant to be a substitute for reading the directory. Some details and recommendations for national and diocesan organizations have not been included in this guide. Hopefully, this book will lead readers to recognize the richness contained in the directory.

The directory represents a new beginning for catechesis in the United States. With this directory the Catholic Church in this country sets forth its understanding of catechetical ministry. It calls on all of us to share the light of our faith. This is the task that remains to be done.

I
What Is Catechesis?

The Name of the Ministry

"That which we call a rose, by any other name would smell as sweet." Quite true. But if the rose did not have a commonly accepted name, we could not talk about it. To talk about it we have to name it.

Different names have been given to that ministry which the directory calls catechesis. These names are important because they describe the way in which the namer perceives the ministry. Twenty-five years ago children in Catholic schools studied "religion." Those who attended a CCD class received "religious instruction." In 1957 Johannes Hofinger, S.J., described this process in the title of his book called *The Art of Teaching Christian Doctrine*. The "catechist" was a teacher of Christian doctrine. The "catechism" was the textbook for this instruction.

Eleven years later, in 1968, Fr. Hofinger published what was called a "Post-Vatican II Edition" of this same book. It was renamed *The Good News and Its Proclamation*. In those intervening eleven years not only had Vatican II occurred, but a series of in-

9

ternational catechetical congresses had been held.
These congresses held in Europe, Africa, Asia, and
South America redefined the nature of the catechetical ministry for the modern Church. The congresses
influenced the Council deliberations and the Council
influenced the congresses. Both events influenced
the writing of the *General Catechetical Directory*
which consistently refers to this ministry as
"catechesis."

The first draft of the United States directory
notes that "In the United States the terms
'catechesis' and 'religious education' are often used
interchangeably by those involved in the educational mission of the Church" (8). It then goes on to
state that these words will be used as synonyms in
this draft.

In the revised draft these two terms are clearly
distinguished and "religious education" is almost
completely dropped from the text. The reason for
this change is stated in article 37 where it notes that
"religious education"

has the advantage of being widely used, but the
disadvantage of standing for so many things
that it lacks precision and clarity. For some it
means academic study about religion divorced
from any call to faith or to religious practice (a
better term might be "religious studies"). For
others it implies a reaction against the efforts of
"Christian education" to initiate people into a
particular religious tradition and religious
community. Still others hold that "religious
education" is solely something that happens in a

classroom and has nothing to do with character formation through education in moral values. For some it is synonymous with theological education; for others with catechetics.

The draft then goes on to state that though it is not essential that one term be used rather than another, "catechesis" will be used in the United States directory because it is used throughout the Catholic world, and because it links us with the rich heritage of the past.

In the consultations many of those responding to the question of this vocabulary, including a number of religious educators, objected to using "catechesis" and "religious education" interchangeably. They also preferred "catechesis" as the term that best describes this particular form of the Church's ministry of the word. In the final text "catechesis" is used throughout the directory. The word catechesis not only more clearly describes the ministry, but it also joins the church in the United States with the other Catholic Churches of the world where this word is almost universally used to describe this ministry.

Catechesis as a Ministry of the Word

The word catechesis is an ancient word which appears often in the documents of the Church. It is derived from a Greek word which means "to resound" or "to sound from above." What is resounded or echoed is the word, the word of the Scriptures and

the Word made flesh. An echo is not a new word. It is
the original word heard in different times and different places. A catechist is one who resounds or
resonates the word of God.

Both the GCD and the NCD note that catechesis
is a form of the ministry of the word. Both directories
note that there are different forms of this ministry,
and that these forms are evangelization, liturgy,
theology, and catechesis. All four forms are closely
related. They differ "depending on circumstances
and on the particular ends in view" (31). They may
be distinguished in theory, yet in practice they are
intimately related.

Evangelization is that form which intends to
arouse the beginnings of faith in unbelievers. It is
the initial proclamation of salvation to persons who
have no knowledge of it or do not yet believe it (35).
This initial proclamation may take the form of the
witness of an authentically Christian life.

The liturgy, especially the liturgy of the word, is
obviously a ministry of the word. In liturgy the
Scriptural word is proclaimed, calling the community to conversion. It is heard and responded to in
song and silence, in prayer of thanks and prayer of
praise. In liturgy the word is also preached. The
homilist opens and interprets in poetry and symbol
the word the community has heard so that the richness of this word may penetrate the hearts of all.
Liturgy is a form of ministry of the word in the context of worship and prayer.

Theology is also a form of this ministry. The
theologians draw on the experience of the community and the word of the Church expressed in
Scripture and taught by the Magisterium of the

Church. These teachings of the Church are reinterpreted and reformulated by theologians so that the good news may always be faithfully proclaimed in a clear and coherent language to each generation. Theologians employ systematic and critical methods, using "philosophy, history, linguistics, and other disciplines in attempting to understand and express Christian truth more clearly" (37).

Catechesis differs from these other forms of the ministry of the word. It differs from evangelization in that it is intended for those who already have the beginnings of faith, even those who "have in fact never given a true personal adherence to the message of revelation" (GCD 18). It differs from liturgy in that it is not worship or response to the word proclaimed in prayer, although such response may be a part of catechesis. It differs from theology in that it is not systematic and scientific study. It does not propose to form theologians, though it does present the verbal expression of the Church's faith.

Catechesis is that form of the ministry of the word in which the faith-community proclaims the word in both verbal and non-verbal ways to both Christian individuals and communities so that all may continue to grow in faith (5). Its fundamental tasks are to share and foster community, to proclaim the mysteries of faith, to motivate to service, and to lead to worship and prayer (32, 39, 213). These four tasks together are the essential components of catechesis. If any one of these components is missing the catechesis is inadequate. Catechesis draws on theology and the human sciences as well as on the total experience of the faith community.

The Purpose of Catechesis

The purpose of catechesis is clearly expressed in the Vatican II document on the *Bishops' Pastoral Role in the Church*. This purpose is repeated in both the GCD and the NCD. Catechesis is that form of the ministry of the word which is intended to make people's "faith become living, conscious, and active through the light of instruction." Catechesis aims at fostering and strengthening faith in believers. This purpose is clearly understood by most Catholics. But tension and controversy arise from different understandings of the meaning of "faith" and "instruction" in this statement.

Prior to Vatican II faith usually referred to the message of revelation as expressed in words. These words were the sacred doctrines or teachings of the Church. These doctrinal formulas or creeds were called *the faith*. "The faith" was understood as being "the content" in the teaching of religion. Faith was preserved by preserving orthodoxy in these teachings. In this light catechesis was primarily an intellectual enterprise. Its aim was to communicate information (the faith). This information when accepted as truth would bring about the formation of Christian character, but catechesis itself was the teaching of Christian doctrine.

Since Vatican II and in the directory, faith is recognized as being loving and total self-surrender to God revealing Himself. It is a way of being. Faith is expressed in all of life. For Christians it is total life-commitment to Christ, the fullness of God's self-revelation. This free surrender to God through Christ in the power of the Spirit is lived out daily. It is expressed in relationships with others, business relationships, familial relationships, community relationships, environmental relationships. Christians place their faith in Christ. They accept Him as Lord of life and the fullness of God's revelation. Faith is the name given to the response of persons in community to God's loving self-donation of Himself. (56-59)

The directory puts these two views of faith, the content of the Christian message and loving response in commitment to God, in perspective (56). It recognizes that the goal of catechesis is to foster that living, conscious, and active faith which is the person's or community's life-response to God's revelation of Himself. This faith the community has articulated in words which express its understanding of this reality. The Sacred Scriptures, creeds and doctrinal formulas are the words in which the Christian community has expressed the mystery of salvation (59). In this sense they are "the faith." Catechesis aims at strengthening faith, a dynamic reality that grows and matures. In so doing it share the scriptures, the creeds and doctrinal formulas which express the faith.

Catechesis is concerned with strengthening the faith described as free response (58), and also unfolding and clarifying the meaning of the message or word in which the Church expresses its faith. If in the past there was what some have described as undue emphasis on the content of faith, apart from the faith of commitment, this imbalance has clearly been corrected in the directory.

The controversy over the purpose of catechesis is also related to the meaning of the word "instruction." The directory notes that "it does not do justice to catechesis to think of it as an instruction alone . . . catechesis is incomplete if it does not take into account the constant interplay between Gospel teaching and human experience, individual and social, personal and institutional, sacred and secular" (35).

This is not a new interpretation of the word "instruction." In the New Testament when Paul uses the Greek word for catechize he clearly distinguishes it from "teaching." To catechize is a technical term used by Paul and in other early Church documents to describe the *way* in which the faith was shared with the catechumens.

For Paul, to catechize meant to teach as Jesus taught. Catechesis was a resounding of the word in such a way that the catechumen was called to a new way of life. The old way had to be uprooted and cast off. Catechesis involved a process where one died to his/her old self and was reborn in the Lord. To catechize was to participate in a life and death enterprise, an enterprise in which all the faithful were involved, calling one another through community, message, service and worship to deepen relationship with the Lord Jesus and His body the Church. To catechize was to foster total adherence to God revealing Himself in Christ, and it included lived out acceptance of the community's expression of that revelation. This is what the directory proposes as the purpose of catechesis. "Catechesis is an esteemed term in Christian tradition" (32). The richness of that tradition has been restored in this directory.

Catechesis is a pastoral activity within the Church and for the Church. At one time the use of the word catechesis was criticized as being too "churchy." Indeed, it is "churchy." In the directory "catechesis" describes a ministry to the Church by the Church. It acknowledges that all of us, always, need to grow in faith. Unless we are a faith-full community we cannot minister to others.

Catechesis is a ministry to the baptized. It is for all believers of every age and every condition in life. It calls for conversion in life from the participants. It is one way in which the Church responds to the Spirit in its midst. It is not the ministry of the Church to the "unchurched" or unbelievers. That ministry is known as evangelization.

Catechesis is for believers. Yet the faith pre-supposed for catechesis is not necessarily mature faith. As the GCD notes, catechesis is directed to those "who have been baptized but lack a proper Christian initiation" (19). It is also directed to those who, "though they belong to the Church, have in fact never given a true personal adherence to the message of revelation" (18). However, catechesis is not for beginners only. It is a "lifelong process," and every form of catechesis "is oriented in some way to the catechesis of adults" (32).

This directory strongly reinforces both the GCD and *To Teach as Jesus Did* in its emphasis on the priority that needs to be given to the catechesis of adults. It repeats the statement of the GCD that adult catechesis is the chief form of catechesis. Perhaps with the hope that this theory may become more than just a theory, the directory recommends that "the catechesis of adults must have high prior-ity at all levels of the Church" (188). If this one guideline is taken seriously, and from the local parish level to the national level, adult catechesis is given "high priority," the Roman Catholic Church in this country will surely be reborn. Since catechesis aims at interior change, at conversion and renewal (35), it seems reasonable to interpret this guideline as a call for the conversion and renewal of the adult Catholic community. The purpose of catechesis may be stated quite briefly: it is the continuing conversion of the faith-community.

The Source and the Signs of Catechesis

If catechesis aims at maturity of faith or continuing conversion for both individuals and communities, where does it begin? What is its source? The directory notes that: "The source of catechesis, which is also its content, is one: God's word, fully revealed in Jesus Christ and active in the lives of people exercising their faith under the guidance of the Magisterium which alone teaches authentically" (41). The source of catechesis is God revealing Himself.

God reveals Himself through His word, written and handed down, that is through Scripture and tradition. This word is manifested and celebrated in the liturgy, in the life of the Church, and "in some way it is known too from those genuine moral values which, by divine providence, are found in human society. Indeed, potentially at least, every instance of God's presence in the world is a source of catechesis" (41).

God revealed and continues to reveal Himself in many words. In the directory these words are called

"signs" or "symbols" of God's self-communication.
Sign, here, is used in the deep sense of sacrament:
That which makes present the reality it symbolizes.

In this sense a sign bears an intimate, not an
accidental, relationship to that which it makes present. It is the expression of the reality it symbolizes.
It is not the same as the reality itself, but *that
through which* we can experience the reality.

Symbols are different from signals. A signal
points to something with which it bears no direct
relationship. For example, red has to be chosen to
say "stop". Another color could have been chosen to
say "stop". Red does not of itself have a direct relationship with "stop". It was arbitrarily chosen to say
"stop".

Symbols are directly related to the reality they
express. For example, when a woman becomes a
mother, she symbolizes her motherhood in her child.
The child makes the woman a mother. There is an
intimate relationship between the woman and the
child. The child is the symbol or expression of the
woman's motherhood.

Signs as sacraments carry meaning. They do not
simply point out something which has no relation to
the symbol itself. They are actual expressions of that
which they symbolize.

Jesus Christ was "the perfect symbol of God on
earth" (114). As Incarnate Son, He is the symbol of
the Father. The Father expresses Himself in the
Son. The Son expresses and makes present the
Father. The Son bears an intimate relationship with
the Father, but is not the same as the Father. He is
the symbol of the Father.

The Church is the symbol or sacrament of the

Risen Christ. It is that through which Christ is present to the world. Through the Church Christ reveals Himself to the world. The Church as symbol makes present in time and space the life of God in Christ for all men and women. Christ expresses Himself through the Church.

The Church as a reality also expresses itself in the symbol. In the early Church the Creed was called *the symbol*. It was recognized as a primary symbol which expressed the Church's meaning. The Church, as symbol of Christ, expresses itself in a variety of signs including its life as a community, the message it proclaims, the service it extends and the worship it offers.

Symbols are full of power. They are also ambiguous. They challenge us to respond to them. They are ordinarily so rich in meaning that we cannot interpret them without help. We need to be initiated into their meaning. Catechesis is a form of the ministry of the word which initiates Christians into the meaning of Christian symbols.

These abiding signs or symbols of God's revelation are classified in the directory under four headings: biblical signs, liturgical signs, ecclesial signs, and natural signs. Although these names closely resemble the four-source method of kerygmatic catechesis of the early 60's (Scripture, liturgy, doctrine, and witness), they are not presented as a methodology and their meaning is much richer. In fact, the entire directory can be seen as a development of these four signs.

The Biblical Signs. The Scriptures are a preeminent expression in word of the Church's experience of God's revelation of Himself. As such they are symbols which make God's revelation present. They are "signs" through which the reality of God's self-revelation may be experienced. They are not only an expression of a past revelation, but they are also a present revelation. Because the Scriptures, like all symbols, are rich in meaning and also ambiguous, they need interpretation. Therefore, in catechesis the community prayerfully studies, reflects on and interprets the biblical signs.

The Liturgical Signs. The liturgical expression of the Church's faith is another experience in which God's presence in the church is expressed through symbol. Sacramental celebrations have rightly been called encounters with Christ. These celebrations symbolize God's presence within and for the community. In sacramental celebration the symbols or symbolic actions express the reality of Christ's saving presence with and for the community. The directory notes that the liturgy and sacramental rites are important signs for catechesis (44). Liturgy and catechesis support each other. Catechesis prepares the members of the community for genuine participation in the liturgy of the Church. Liturgy as an expression of faith and a continuing re-creation of faith ideally calls forth a desire for continuing catechesis on the mysteries which the community celebrates.

The Ecclesial Signs. The Church itself is a sacrament or symbol of the Risen Lord (63, 97). As such its whole life is a sign for catechesis. The life of the Church includes its nature as a community, its ded-

ication to service, and the message through which it
articulates or expresses its faith. Its life is also expressed in common worship and prayer. This ritual
expression of life is so significant however, that it is
treated as that special expression of life call liturgical. The Church's life is also expressed in individual
members of the faith community.

The Natural Signs. God reveals Himself through
creation, through human beings, and through
human cultures (51). These are all symbols or "natural signs" of His presence. The Church's prophetic
mission requires that she examine these natural
signs and interpret them in the light of the Gospel.
In fact, the directory notes that catechesis "has the
task of examining at the most profound level the
meaning and value of everything created, including
the products of human effort, in order to show how
all creation sheds light on the mystery of God's saving power and is in turn illuminated by it" (46).
These are the natural signs of God's revelation.

These are the four signs or symbols of the one
source of catechesis, God revealing Himself to
humankind. It is the task of catechesis to reflect on
these signs, the Scriptures, the Church, the liturgy,
creation and human experience, and to interpret
them. Through catechesis the community and individuals ask, in the light of these signs, "What is the
meaning of life?" "What is the meaning of Christian
life?"

These signs are so central and so significant in
the directory that the whole of the document can be
seen as a reflection on the meaning of these four

signs for the Christian community. They are the unifying themes around which all the guidelines are gathered.

For this reason, the remaining chapters of this book are organized around the four signs of catechesis. A final chapter on the catechist has been added primarily because this book is written for catechists. By centering on these signs we hope to bring together from the various parts of the directory the main points that it makes about each sign.

Study Questions on Catechesis

1. Name some of the forms which evangelization, liturgy, theology, and catechesis take at the local level.

2. Do you think some of the misunderstandings and confused expectations of catechetical programs stem from a lack of awareness of what catechesis is and is not? Cite examples. How can this be remedied?

3. What are the four fundamental tasks of catechesis? How should these be considered when evaluating catechetical programs? Do you think most Catholics are aware of the goals of catechesis? What can happen at the local level to make them more aware of these general goals as well as the specific goals of a particular program?

4. Recalling only what you remember from your grade school education, how would you define

faith? How has faith been talked about since Vatican II? How would you define faith now? Is it difficult to move from a static view of faith to a more dynamic one? What are some of the problems?

5. Throughout many Church documents, including the NCD, special emphasis has been given to adult catechesis. How can we begin to give the catechesis of adults a high priority? Brainstorm about the areas of need for adult education in your local area.

6. Name some important signs or symbols in your life. Cite as well as you can the meaning associated with the sign or symbol. Why are symbols important? Do you agree with the idea that the most meaningful and intimate relationship of our lives can only be expressed symbolically? If so, cite examples.

7. What is the importance of understanding signs or symbols in the world of catechesis?

8. Name some of the signs that come to your mind under the following headings:
   A. Biblical signs
   B. Liturgical signs
   C. Ecclesial signs
   D. Natural signs

II
The Biblical Signs

Most adults in the Roman Catholic Church did not experience, as children, a scriptural catechesis; and until recently there has not been much catechesis on the Bible for adults. However, this is changing. The directory recognizes as a positive factor in today's Church that many Catholics are expressing a renewed interest in the Bible (9).

During the past two decades developments in biblical scholarship have been shared with the general public through books and magazine articles. Authors of catechetical materials have frequently incorporated these insights into their catechetical programs. The liturgical renewal has also aided us to become more familiar with the Scriptures.

Although the directory does not have a chapter on the Bible, guidelines on the biblical signs permeate the entire document. The directory incorporates catechesis on the scriptural sign in every chapter except the final one which considers catechetical resources. What does it say about catechesis on the biblical signs?

The Bible as Sign of Revelation

The term "biblical sign," according to the directory, "refers to the varied and wonderful ways, recorded in Scripture, by which God reveals Himself" (43). The Bible as symbol is a *present* revelation. The Scriptures are not only an account of a past revelation, but are also one of the means which keep God's presence before us in today's world.

This present revelation of God through the Bible is not magic, nor is it mechanical. God is revealing Himself in the Scriptures to the believing community through the medium of human language.

All language is symbolic. Through language we express ourselves and make ourselves present to others. We sing to express our feelings; we write a grocery list to keep some facts, an empty refrigerator, in mind. We write love letters both to express ourselves and to communicate our feelings to our beloved. All verbal expressions are symbolic, but all do not have the same importance. A grocery list is not as significant as a love letter.

A love letter is a symbol. It is that through which a person expresses himself or herself. Through such a letter the writer is made present to the beloved. The letter is not the same as the love of the writer, but it is a way of overcoming separation. It makes the lover present to the beloved.

Language is always limited in that it does not express everything we are trying to say. No words can express the fullness of human love, though poets and lovers have attempted to do so for centuries. But words can express deep human feelings and desires.

They can, more or less adequately, make us present to one another.

When love is expressed in a letter and is mutual, the receiver of the letter is moved by it. This response is not simply or primarily intellectual. The whole person, intellectually, emotionally, physically, rejoices. The beloved is challenged to respond to the love offered. The beloved is changed.

The Bible is like a love letter. It was written by persons within the believing community who had experienced God's revelation of himself. These writers, inspired by the Holy Spirit, symbolized this experience in language. Through the medium of human language God's loving revelation of Himself is communicated. Through this human language, God makes Himself known and present to us. The Bible is not the same as the God who reveals Himself through it. But through the Bible God's revelation is communicated.

Like a love letter the Scriptures were written for a responding community. Like a love letter they express and make present a reality beyond themselves. Like a love letter they leave something unsaid, they excite the imagination, call forth a response, and challenge the depth of the love relationship.

Unlike a love letter the Bible is not always easy to read. Its earliest texts were written almost three thousand years ago. Even the New Testament is almost two thousand years old. These writings reflect the culture and the time in which they were written. Some parts of it, such as the first eleven chapters of Genesis, are written in a literary form with which we are not familiar. For these reasons the commu-

nity needs help in interpreting the scriptures, as
well as accurate and readable translations.

The scriptures were composed and assembled by
the community under the inspiration of the Holy
Spirit. The community of old, Israel and the Apostolic Church, handed on these holy writings to future generations "as testimony to their beliefs and
their experience of grace." The receiving and present
believing community, which is also experiencing
God's self-revelation in other ways, is challenged to
change its way of life when it reads or listens to the
scriptures. Reflection on the scriptures in order to
penetrate their meaning more deeply is one of the
tasks of catechesis. (43)

The Biblical Signs in Catechesis

The biblical signs of God revealing Himself
which are recorded in scripture are not all of equal
significance. There is a hierarchy in these signs.

The directory points out three "chief signs"
which are "to be emphasized in all catechesis" (43).
The first sign is the "creation account, which culmi-
nates in the establishment of God's kingdom." Creation is not a once-upon-a-time, static event. It did
not simply happen in the past. It continues even
now.

The second chief sign is the covenant, beginning
with Abraham and his descendants and reaching
fulfillment in "God's new covenant in Jesus Christ
which is extended to all people." The covenant, also,
is recognized as a present event.

The third great sign is the Exodus. The Exodus

includes the passage from bondage to freedom recorded in the Old Testament as well as "the parallel,
but far more profound, passage from death to life
accomplished by Christ's paschal mystery." "Underlying all as an authentic biblical sign is the community of believers—the People of Israel, the Church,"
from whom these writings came. (43).

A catechesis on the biblical signs is much more
than a sharing of information about biblical events
and persons. In biblical catechesis the Church reflects on the vision of life which the communities
and writers of the scriptures experienced. As symbols of God's presence, the scriptures make present
God's word to us today. Biblical catechesis fosters a
growing consciousness of God's loving and creative
activity in our present lives. It leads to a deepening
recognition of the covenant bond which we freely
choose to embrace today. It helps us to recognize the
painful events in life as our sharing in the death-
resurrection exodus of Christ.

As these signs show, the directory presents the
themes of the Old and New Testaments as a unified
whole. It notes, however, that the "books of the New
Testament, especially the gospels, enjoy pre-emi-
nence as principal witness of the life and teaching of
Jesus" (60).

The directory acknowledges that there is more
than one theology in the New Testament (16). For
example, the gospel of John begins with the proclamation of the pre-existence or divinity of Jesus,
while Mark structures his gospel around a progres-
sive revelation of Jesus as Messiah and Son of God.
The Church is also represented differently. John
presents an unstructured church, while Paul and the

Pastoral Epistles write of a highly organized community. These differing theologies are not contradictory, but complementary. They reflect the varied experiences and insights of the Christian communities and the writers. They reflect our own varied experiences and insights.

The Biblical Signs and the Catechized

Because the Gospels are pre-eminent among the writings in the scriptures, and because Jesus is the "supreme expression" of God's revelation, so catechesis should acquaint "everyone, according to ability . . . with the infancy narratives, the miracles and parables of Jesus' public life, and the accounts of His passion, death and resurrection" (60).

A refrain that is consistently repeated in the directory is that in all catechizing, the age, circumstances of life, and ability of those being catechized are to be considered. Necessary adaptations are to be made because of these factors (39; 176; 177; 180, 4, 6, 9, 12, 13; 200; 229; etc.).

The directory recognizes that pre-school children, view the world "in very concrete terms drawn from direct personal experiences," but as they grow, 6-10, their "ability to form abstract ideas or concepts based on experience increases" (178). It notes that during this age-period (6-10) stories like the parables have meaning for the children.

Article 176e, which is on formulations, notes that children, presumably those from 6-13, should have certain "factual information" which contributes "to an appreciation of the place of the Word of

God in the Church and the life of the Christian."
This includes an awareness and understanding of
the key themes of the history of salvation (creation,
covenant, exodus, community), the major per-
sonalities of the Old Testament such as Abraham,
Moses, David, and the prophets and the New Testament, Jesus, the Twelve, Mary, Paul, and certain
biblical texts expressive of God's love and care. This
information "should be adapted to the level and
ability of the child and introduced in a gradual
manner, through a process which, begun early, continues gradually, flexibly, and never slavishly."

Rememberance should never be cheapened or
vulgarized to mean only memorization. Remembering enables us to have a past and to share a past
with others. Our own identity, who we are, is depen-
dent on our past. As Christians we share a common
heritage. Through biblical catechesis we recognize
the biblical heritage as our own.

In referring to pre-adolescents, ages 10-13, the
directory points out that this is a time when a topic
like "the nature of Scripture" can be discussed (179).
This reference seems to refer to a study of how the
scriptures came into being and the literary forms of
the varied writings. It emphasizes the importance of
reflecting on the meaning of the scriptures so they
can be seen as related to our lives.

The directory notes that there is a decline
among youth or adolescents (those over 13) in their
acceptance of the Bible as God's word (200c). For
some of these youth there is "confusion concerning
the language and thought of the Bible" (200e). It
recommends that the study of scripture be part of
the overall catechesis of these youth, so that the

problems they have with the scriptures may be met (228b).

While the directory is ordinarily not specific regarding what concepts should be included in adolescent biblical catechesis, the guideline given in paragraph 60i would seem to apply to them. In this article the directory specifies that "catechesis explains the number and structure of the books of the Old and New Testaments, speaks of them as God's inspired word, and treats their major themes, such as creation, salvation, and final fulfillment.

The directory points out that during the period of early adulthood, which it considers as being between the ages of 18 and 35 (182), catechesis should continue to present scripture and encourage reflection on it. "The gradual manner of God's self-revelation, manifested in scripture, provides a model for catechetical efforts directed to young adults" (227). Through catechesis the Church should encourage young adults "to listen to God's word in community" (227). There is frequent reference throughout the directory to the use of the Bible as a source of prayer for all age groups (43, 141, 142, 143).

It is adults who are more fully able to comprehend and respond to God's word. As the directory gives prime place to the catechesis of adults, so it also recommends that scripture be an integral part of adult catechesis (185, 188, 243). It is in adult catechesis that "the work of biblical scholars is studied, as a means to achieving 'deeper insight into the sense intended by God speaking through the sacred writer' " (60i). Catechesis on the biblical sign is always related to the living of Christian life.

The scriptures, as a sign of catechesis, are intimately related to the liturgical, ecclesial, and natural signs. One important criterion for the evaluation of catechetical programs is the integration of all four signs into the catechesis.

The Biblical Signs and the Tasks of Catechesis

The fundamental tasks of catechesis are to proclaim the message, to build community, to lead to worship and prayer and to motivate to service. Catechesis on the biblical signs is one way of carrying out these tasks.

Catechesis on the biblical signs builds community. It puts the community in touch with its past and enables it to understand its own identity as Church. The directory notes that the nature and mission of the Church "are best captured in scriptural parables and images taken from ordinary life, which not only express truth about its nature but challenge the Church" (63). For example, the scriptures present the Church as the people of God (64), one Body of Christ (65), as servant (66), as a sign of the kingdom (67), and a pilgrim Church (68). Catechesis on these images enables the community to reflect on its present mission and identity. It challenges the Church to be more faithful to its calling. It reminds the Church of what it ought to be. In so doing it builds community.

The scriptures are a proclamation of the Christian message. The message cannot be fully proclaimed apart from the scriptures. If one studies chapter five in the directory, which considers the

Christian message, this becomes quite clear.
Scriptural references abound. These references are
not used as "proof texts," but point out that the message is intimately related to the scripture as its
source.

Catechesis on the biblical signs calls individuals
and the community to service. "Powerful and com-
pelling bases for the Church's social ministry" are
found "throughout the Bible, especially in the Old
Testament covenants and prophets, and in the Gospels and some epistles in the New Testament" (151).
Who can reflect on the Sermon on the Mount or the
Beatitudes without recognizing Christ's call for
commitment to social justice? The prophets, especially Isaiah and Amos, remind the community of its
present responsibility to care for the poor, for
widows and orphans.

Catechesis on the Bible leads to a fuller participation in liturgy. Such catechesis "fosters informed
participation in the liturgy by helping people recognize biblical themes and language which are part of
the readings and sacramental rites" (43). The
Church today prays through symbolic actions which
come out of our biblical roots. We continue to walk
through the water, anoint with oil, and gather to
celebrate the holy meal. Biblical catechesis helps us
to recognize the deep meaning of these actions.

Catechesis on the biblical sign is a call to respond to God's word of revelation by a conversion of
heart. It fosters the faith of individuals and communities. The directory recognizes our need for such
catechesis and suggests many ways in which catechists may carry out this part of their ministry.

Study Questions on the Biblical Signs

1. What are some of the biblical signs by which God has revealed Himself to people? What do these signs tell us about ourselves, about our relationship to our neighbor and God?

2. What opportunities are presently available for further study of the scriptures?

3. A person's deepest longings, emotions and relationships often can be expressed only by use of symbols. Name some verbal and non-verbal symbols.

4. What are some symbols of love you have received throughout life—your early life, school years, adolescence, young adult years and adult years?

5. Why is it fitting to speak as the Bible does about God's relationship to persons and people's response to God in terms of symbol?

6. The dynamic power of creation is still at work today. What are some signs of this?

7. We read in scripture of God's covenant (ritual promise) with Abraham (Gen. 12, 1-9) and Moses (Ex. 3, 1-15) and the new covenant of Christ Jesus (Lk. 22, 19-20 or Mt. 20, 26-29). Is God calling us to a covenant relationship to each other? to Him? What are some of the signs of this?

8. The Exodus is a story of pain and hardship leading to freedom and new life. What are some present day Exodus experiences in political life, family life, personal life?

9. In Judeo-Christian traditions there has often been more than one acceptable point of view or practice. The Gospels give evidence of this. Why is this important to the faith of the Church? Does diversity mean disunity?

10. Why is it important to keep the age and religious readiness of a child in mind when presenting biblical signs?

11. How do we pray using scripture?

12. The goal of catechesis is to foster mature faith. Are there different ways of expressing faith in Jesus and His mission? Cite examples from the Gospels. How can diversity in the expression of faith not take away from the unity of faith but rather enrich the faithful community?

Articles in the NCD that refer to the Biblical Signs						
Preface	Chapter 1	Chapter 2	Chapter 3	Chapter 4	Chapter 5	Chapter 6
5	16	34	52	63	83	121
9		38	53	66	85	141
		42	55	70	86	142
		43	59	72	104	
		45	60	73	105	
		47		74		
				77		

	Chapter 7	Chapter 8	Chapter 9	Chapter 10	Chapter 11	
	150	176	207	223		
	155	178	211	225		
	156	179	213	227		
	163	183	214	228		
	170	185	216	234		
		200	217	241		
				242		
				243		

III
The Liturgical Signs

"Catechesis for a Worshiping Community," chapter 6 in the directory, is the longest chapter in the document. It has thirty-six articles which are grouped under four major headings: liturgy and catechesis, the sacraments/mysteries, prayer, and sacred art and sacramentals.

What Is Liturgy?

Liturgy is the prayer or worship of the community. In liturgy the community expresses its faith in actions (59). Liturgy is the community's ritual celebration of Christian life. Liturgy springs out of faith, a faith which recognizes that God is at work in people's lives, a faith that compels Christians to respond to Him. Faith is a way of life which begs to express itself in the prayer of the community. For the faithful person worship is a necessity of life. "Faith brings the community together to worship; and in worship faith is renewed" (112).

What does the faith-community do in worship? "It praises God for His goodness and glory. It also

39

acknowledges its total dependence on God, the
Father, and accepts the gift of divine life which He
wishes to share with us in the Son, through the out-
pouring of the Spirit. Worship creates, expresses,
and fulfills the Church. It is the action in and by
which men and women are drawn into the mystery
of the glorified Christ" (112).

Liturgy is the worship of the community. It is
distinguished from private prayer which may be
worship but is not community worship. All sacramental celebrations are community worship. It has
become common to describe those community prayer
services which are not sacramental as *para*liturgies
or scriptural celebrations. The directory points out
that although these are not substitutes for the official liturgy of the Church, "they can deepen faith,
strengthen community, foster Christian love, lead to
more ardent and fruitful participation in sacramental celebration, and intensify the community's commitment to social justice" (142). For this reason they
are examined together with the official worship of
the Church.

Over the centuries the Church has always been
a worshiping community, but sometimes it has
changed its ritual way of expressing its faith. For
example, in the apostolic Church and for many centuries thereafter Baptism was ritualized by immer-
sion of the person in water. There have been a
number of significant changes in our ritual expression of worship since the Second Vatican Council.
Recognizing that catechists seldom have an opportunity to study the official rites, though they do experience them, the directory presents a brief expla-
nation of each sacramental rite that is based on the
new revised rituals. The directory does not attempt

to provide a full sacramental theology. It acknowledges recent changes in the Church's liturgy and
points out the catechetical implications of such
changes.

Throughout this chapter there are many references to the liturgical traditions of the Eastern
Churches. For those catechists who are not familiar
with the Eastern Churches these references are
helpful in two ways. They present the different traditions within some of these churches, and are a re-
minder that there are now and always have been
different liturgical traditions within the Church.
Article 15 notes that:

Over the centuries the Eastern and Western
Churches have developed diverse traditions,
theologies, liturgies, and forms of spirituality,
all faithful expressions of the teachings of
Christ. Representing cultures and world views
with which most Catholics in this country are
not familiar, the Eastern Churches provide significant alternative resources for catechesis.
The insights of all the traditions are needed to
deal with the varieties of pluralism in the
United States.

Catechesis and Liturgy

Catechesis and liturgy are closely related. Both
are ministries for and by the community; both
strengthen faith. But each has its own specific identity. They are inseparably linked, but each had a
different purpose.

Catechesis leads to worship. "It prepares people

for full and active participation in liturgy by helping
them understand the nature, rituals, and symbols of
the liturgy. Catechesis strengthens faith, which
faith then expresses itself in prayer. At the same
time it flows from liturgy in as much as worship
leads the community to desire a fuller catechesis"
(113). "Liturgy and catechesis support each other.
Prayer and the sacraments call for informed participants; fruitful participation in catechesis calls for
the spiritual enrichment that comes from liturgical
participation" (36).

Catechesis leads to liturgy but the liturgy is not
a catechetical tool:

> While every liturgical celebration has educative
> and formative value, liturgy should not be
> treated as subservient to catechesis. On the con-
> trary, catechesis should "promote an active,
> conscious, genuine participation in the liturgy
> of the Church, not merely by explaining the
> meaning of ceremonies, but also by forming the
> minds of the faithful for prayer, for thanksgiv-
> ing, for repentance, for praying with confidence,
> for a community spirit and for understanding
> correctly the meaning of the creeds" (36).

The Sacraments/Mysteries As Symbol (114)

The significance of the introductory paragraph
on the sacraments cannot be overemphasized. It is
itself a verbal catechesis on the meaning of symbol
of which we have already written a great deal. A
symbol is that through which a reality is made pres-

ent. This paragraph points out that "the Word of God is the full manifestation of the Father; thus He may be called a symbol (image, icon) of the Father." Jesus as symbol challenges us to response, to conversion, to faith.

The sacraments are symbolic actions of the Church that is the symbol of Christ. They are, therefore, acts of Christ and the Church. As symbolic actions they call for response, that is, they "effect what they symbolize" (114). One should never say "only a symbol," for these symbols embody and re-present the saving acts of Christ for and in the Church.

Sacraments of Initiation (115)

The sacraments of initiation are, Baptism, Confirmation, and Eucharist, through them "a person is incorporated into the Church and shares its mission in the world." Initiation into the Church occurs in stages, as the candidate successively participates in the rite of initiation. The directory notes that the new Rite of Christian Initiation of Adults provides "a norm for catechetical as well as pastoral practice in this regard." These three sacraments are intimately related and this relationship should be emphasized in catechesis.

One aspect of this relationship which catechists may note is the recognition that faith is not a static reality given in Baptism. Adult candidates are baptized because of the faith they already possess. Infants are baptized because of the faith of their parents. Becoming a Christian with mature faith is a process that goes on throughout life. It begins as one enters the church, but the beginning is not the end. Faith grows to maturity. Mature faith cannot be expected of children or adolescents. Faith continues growing throughout life.

The Rite of Christian Initiation of Adults is presented as both a norm and a model for all sacramental catechesis. This means that all sacramental catechesis involves a community of catechists, who support, pray, reflect, instruct, witness, serve and proclaim with the candidates. Preparing candidates for the sacraments of initiation in this rite is a catechetical process and a liturgical experience. Catechetically, the community is responsible for the catechesis which takes many forms. Liturgically, it prays with and prepares liturgies which symbolize the candidates' growth in faith. In the process both candidate and community are called to continuing conversion in life.

Baptism (116-117)

The theology of the sacrament of Baptism focuses on three aspects of the meaning of this sacrament. First it states in theological terms that through Baptism we become children of God, sharers in divine life, and are cleansed from original sin. The second point emphasizes the traditional understanding that through Baptism we "are initiated and welcomed into the community of faith." The third point is that through Baptism all share in Christ's priesthood, and so all the faithful are called "to minister both to the community of faith and the whole world."

The section on catechesis for Baptism focuses on

adults. It is adults, those who are candidates for
Baptism, parents of infants to be baptized, and godparents, toward whom catechesis for Baptism is
primarily directed. This catechesis ought also to involve the community of the faithful, that is, the local
parish, who support the catechized by prayer and
witness.

Baptismal catechesis is Trinitarian. It centers on
the Father's love, the life-death-resurrection of the
Son, and the gift of the Spirit to the Church. It is also
experiential in character. The candidate for baptism
needs to experience the Christian community as a
faith-full, worshipping, serving, and supporting
community. It also includes experience of and reflection on the meaning of the ritual, symbols (water,
oil, light, the community), and the symbolic actions
in sacramental celebration.

The text includes the statement that "children
should not be deprived of Baptism." However, it
strongly emphasizes the need for catechesis of parents and godparents before the Baptism of infants,
so that they may "re-examine the meaning which
faith has in their lives."

Confirmation (118-119)

Possibly there is no sacrament for which it is
more difficult to catechize than the sacrament of
Confirmation. Presently, in different parts of the
United States, children are confirmed before age
seven and at every age thereafter, including the college years. The directory acknowledges this when it
states that "practice in this matter now varies so

much among the dioceses of the United States, that
it is impossible to prescribe a single catechesis for
this sacrament." This pastoral practice reflects a
certain lack of consensus among theologians and
liturgical specialists about the sacrament, which in
turn creates difficulties for catechists. The confusion
is acknowledged but has not been resolved in the
directory.

The directory states that Confirmation/Chris-
mation is a sacrament of initiation, and as such it is
intimately related to Baptism and the Eucharist.
Christians are strengthened by Confirmation.
"Specifically, in Confirmation/Chrismation they are
signed with the gift of the Spirit and become more
perfect images of their Lord." Confirmation calls the
Christian to bear witness, and to work eagerly for
the building up of Christ's Body.

All agree that Confirmation is a sacrament of
initiation, and the directory reiterates this in several articles. But the meaning of the word "initiation" is interpreted differently. "In the Eastern
Churches, Baptism and Chrismation (Confirmation)
are celebrated together in infancy and their intimate relationship is apparent." Those who see initiation as a process that goes on until the youngster is
able to commit him or herself fully to Christ and the
Church postpone Confirmation until a later date,
perhaps even early adulthood.

Catechists who are asked to prepare children of
grade school age for Confirmation are presently
given an unenviable task. On what theology of Confirmation are they to base their catechesis? Are
pre-adolescents ready to confirm their Baptism?
Does the community have the right to accept or re-

ject them? On what basis? The dilemma facing many
catechists has not, and it seems cannot, yet be resolved.

The directory does suggest a catechesis based on
commitment. It notes that appropriate catechesis for
different age youngsters is being done and that this
catechesis includes: "performance standards for
Church membership and community service; re-
questing a specified number of hours of service
to qualify for Confirmation; a letter of request
for Confirmation; formational programs of catechesis extending over two or three years; and
the use of adult advisors." Again it repeats, as in
Baptism, that the parish community "has an obliga-
tion to participate in the catechetical preparation of
those to be confirmed." And parents and sponsors
are "to be intimately involved in catechesis for Confirmation."

The Eucharist (120-121)

"The Eucharist is the center and heart of Christian life." It is so central and so significant that it is
not possible to write about it adequately. But as
there is a time when one must try to describe a personal love in words, so there is a time when we need
to try to put into words what the Eucharist means.
The words are abstract. What is being talked about
is that very human celebration in which Christians
express and renew their identity as Church.

"It is a traditional theme of both the Eastern
and Western Churches, that Eucharist forms
Church." The Eucharist is a sign and cause of unity.

It builds up the body which is the Church. It expresses the unity of believers. The directory states quite clearly that the Church is meant to be a Eucharistic community, the Body of Christ. One of the strong points in the directory is its emphasis on the sacraments as communal actions which strengthen the unity and faith of the community. This is quite evident in the section on the Eucharist.

The directory also states that "all that belongs to Christian life leads to the eucharistic celebration or flows from it." The Sunday Eucharist is not an isolated moment in life, separated from daily experiences. It is that moment when the community comes together with its joys and pain, its failures and successes to join with one another and Christ to offer thanksgiving to the Father.

"The Eucharist is a memorial of the Lord's passion, death, and resurrection." A memorial is a remembering. In remembering, the past is actualized in the present. Through memory the past becomes contemporaneous. In the Eucharist as memorial we participate in the passion, death, resurrection of the Lord.

The Eucharist is a "holy sacrifice." It is a sacrifice of praise and thanksgiving. In the Eucharist we commemorate Christ's gift of himself to the father. With Christ and in his name we surrender ourselves as body of Christ to the Father. We share the cup and bread which memoralize Christ's sacrificial death for us.

"The Eucharistic celebration is a holy meal," a sacred banquet. It is the holy meal of the community in which the community celebrates its identity as Body of Christ. As friends and family celebrate birthdays, or special anniversaries or holidays, so the Christian community gathers together to celebrate its faith and life in Christ in the Eucharist. As Christ celebrated His life in a covenant meal with His friends, so the community gathers together to recall that Last Supper and to celebrate Christ present in its midst. With bread and wine we gather around the scared table. With Christ we offer the great prayer of thanksgiving over the bread and cup. As he broke the bread and shared the cup with his disciples, so we share them with one another.

"The Eucharist is also a sacrament of reconciliation, completing and fulfilling the sacraments of initiation." The directory reminds us of a truth that has frequently been missing in eucharistic catechesis. According to St. Thomas the Eucharist is the primary sacrament of reconciliation. The custom of believing it is necessary to receive the sacrament of Penance, even when not in serious sin, before receiving Communion is evidence of a lack of appreciation of the Eucharist as a sacrament of reconciliation. "The Eucharist proclaims and effects our reconciliation with the Father. 'Look with favor on your Church's offering, and see the Victim whose death has reconciled us to yourself.' "

In a few paragraphs the directory summarizes some high points of eucharistic theology. It does not and could not present a full eucharistic theology. However, it stimulates to further reflection on this mystery.

But how does one catechize for the Eucharist? The first paragraph in article 121 on "Catechesis for the Eucharist" notes that catechesis recognizes the Eucharist as the heart of Christian life and "helps people understand that celebration of the Eucharist nourishes the faithful with Christ, the Bread of Life, in order that, filled with the love of God and neighbor, they may become more and more a people acceptable to God and build up the Christian community with works of charity, service, missionary activity, and witness."

Catechesis for the Eucharist also reflects on "Christ's life as proclaimed in the gospels." It considers "the Last Supper and the Jewish roots of this covenant meal." The reality of presence and the meaning of symbol need to be reflected on so that the catechized will understand the presence of Christ in the community, in His word as proclaimed in the Eucharist, and in the bread and wine.

Catechesis for the Eucharist will "also help people understand the importance and significance of the liturgy of the word in the eucharistic celebration." Every sacrament begins with the proclamation of the word. This word challenges each member of the community to live the Christian life more fully. It calls to conversion and deepened faith. Insight into the meaning of the scriptural passages through catechesis prepares us to respond to the word proclaimed in the Eucharist.

All of the recommendations for catechesis for the Eucharist should be read with an understanding of the catechetical process. It is a life-long endeavor. Everything cannot and should not be attempted at once. When catechizing children the principle that the catechist always considers the age, capacity, and experience of the child will determine the form and content of the catechesis.

Article 176e notes that children should at some

point memorize the parts of the Mass. According to the *General Instruction* of the Roman Missal the parts of the Mass are the liturgy of the word and liturgy of the Eucharist. In addition the Mass has introductory and concluding rites. They should also memorize "the various eucharistic devotions." Eucharistic devotions mentioned are Holy Hours, Benediction, visits of adoration, the Forty Hours Devotion, Corpus Christi, and First Friday eucharistic devotions (143).

First Communion (122)

This article focuses on children's preparation for First Communion. It notes that the preparation of adults for First Communion is an integral part of the catechumenate process.

Parents, catechists, and pastors "are responsible for determining when they (children) are ready to receive First Communion." In many places in the directory the rights and duties of parents as primary catechists or educators of their children are clearly defined. Parents have both a "right and duty to be intimately involved in preparing their children for First Communion." In parishes where this pastoral practice is already a reality this custom has been ratified. Where such a practice is not a reality, it is quite clear that it ought to be so.

Suggestions for catechesis for First Communion include the three recommendations set up by Pius X: children should be aware of the main events of Christ's life, they should recognize that the Eucharist is not ordinary bread but is the Body of

Christ, and they should desire to receive it.

Catechesis for First Communion should be based on the experiences of the child. It is to be "conducted separately from introductory catechesis for the Sacrament of Reconciliation, since each sacrament deserves its own concentrated preparation." The directory recommends continuing catechesis on the Eucharist for children as they grow and mature. It notes that "in some Eastern Churches in the United States, First Communion completes an infant's reception of the sacraments of initiation, Baptism and Chrismation" (Confirmation). Therefore, eucharistic catechesis will also follow the reception of the sacrament.

The Eucharistic Liturgy for Groups with Special Needs (134-139)

This section of chapter six does not follow immediately after the articles on the Eucharist in the directory. But since the catechetical guidelines it recommends (139) fit all catechesis for the Eucharist, it shall be considered here. This section includes suggestions for eucharistic celebrations for smaller groups, children, youth, cultural groups, and those persons with handicapping conditions.

It points out that "ordinarily the parish Sunday Mass is the community celebration which reflects and shapes the lives of parishioners." However, occasionally, there are good reasons for Masses for smaller groups whose members have special bonds in common. These Masses lead to a deeper appreciation of the unity symbolized and effected by the eucharistic celebration in the larger community. These celebrations should be adapted to the nature of the group (age, maturity, race, cultural or ethnic group, and handicap) according to the norms and guidelines of the official liturgical books. This adaptation can be of varied nature as is clear from the recommendations made for adapting children's Masses in the *Directory for Masses with Children* issued by the Sacred Congregation for Divine Worship in 1973.

Catechists are frequently called upon by smaller groups to help them plan and prepare liturgies. They should encourage persons to participate actively and to accept the ministerial roles open to them. Cultural, racial, or ethnic groups have "the right to use their own language and cultural expressions of faith in ritual, music, art." Catechists may guide them in doing this.

In order to help others plan and prepare for liturgies, catechists themselves should have adequate liturgical preparation, both theoretical and practical. Parishes and diocesan offices are asked to provide catechists with opportunities for liturgical celebrations, prayer, retreats and other experiences of Christian community with others engaged in this ministry (213). Colleges and universities are encouraged to offer courses in liturgy (242) which will enable catechists to have a deeper insight into the mysteries. However, since the Eucharist itself is the special sign of unity and cause of growth in faith within the community, "the catechist needs to experience this unity through frequent participation in the celebration of the Eucharist with other catechists and with those being catechized" (209). Par-

ticipation in the Eucharist challenges the faithful to
minister to others. The ministry of catechesis is one
form of response to this challenge.

Sacraments/Mysteries of Reconciliation and Healing

The Sacrament of Reconciliation (124-125)

By participating in the Sacrament of Reconciliation Christians express the "continuing process of
conversion" (99) which is going on in their lives.
Conversion is "a profound change of the whole person by which one begins to consider, judge and ar-
range one's whole life to conform more with Christ's
values."

This sacrament both expresses and signifies reconciliation. It symbolizes our reconciliation with
God and with the Church. Sinners who experience
forgiveness and reconciliation in this sacrament
"are signs of the Church as a healing community"
(45).

The directory explains briefly the three ways in
which this sacrament is celebrated. The directory
notes that communal celebrations symbolize more
clearly the ecclesial or community nature of the sacrament. It points out that in the rite for individual
penitents the penitent should have the choice of
anonymity or a face-to-face setting with the priest. It
refers to the form of general absolution, simply noting
that it is to be celebrated according to the norms
given in articles 31 and 32 of the Rite of Penance.

Catechesis for this sacrament recognizes that participation in it is an expression of Christian life. Faith as a call to conversion from sin is a prerequisite for the sacrament.

Catechesis for Reconciliation emphasizes the mercy of God and His loving forgiveness and challenges people to examine their lives in the light of the Gospel. Catechesis prepares the community to celebrate the realities of repentance, conversion and reconciliation.

Catechesis of Children for Reconciliation (126)

The controversy over when children should first celebrate this sacrament was evident throughout the preparation of this article. When the directory was discussed at the bishops' meeting in November 1977, seven amendments which would have clarified it one way or another were presented. Six were either rejected or withdrawn. Only one amendment was accepted for this article. The letter from the Sacred Congregation for the Clergy which approved the directory also added a suggestion regarding its content. This suggestion was incorporated into the final version of the directory.

Although the writers of the directory attempted to exise the words "must" and "should" from the text whenever possible, this article begins with the words, "Catechesis for children must always respect the natural disposition, ability, age and circumstance of individuals." It also states that parents should be involved in the preparation of their children for the sacrament. The word preparation was deliberately chosen to replace catechesis in this case in order to emphasize the pre-eminent rights of parents to decide when their children are ready to celebrate the sacrament.

The article notes that parents should be involved in the catechesis of their children for this sacrament. It also notes that "Catechesis for the Sacrament of Reconciliation is to precede First Communion and must be kept distinct by a clear and unhurried separation." This *catechesis* is to precede and be separate from First Communion so that "the specific identity of each sacrament is apparent and so that, before receiving First Communion, the child will be familiar with the revised Rite of Reconciliation and will be at ease with the reception of the sacrament." The document from Rome recommended adding a statement which points out that the sacrament of reconciliation should "*normally*" be celebrated prior to the reception of first communion. This was done. It is interesting to note that the Sacred Congregation itself used the qualifying word *normally*. Even Rome does not issue an absolute time, without qualification, as some dioceses and parishes in the United States presently do, either in theory or practice.

Parents have the right and therefore should have the option, in practice, of deciding if and when their children are prepared to celebrate this sacrament. How can they exercise this right if peer pressure or parish pressure as expressed in parish practice exclude it? How can they exercise it if there are no structural options which permit such a decision?

It may be that many or most or some parents will decide that their children are ready before first communion. Others may decide that their children are not ready. Do our present diocesan and/or parish structures enable them to make this decision freely? Coercion in such a matter, whether subtle or blatant, is a very serious infringement on parental rights. The Roman Congregation felt that it was necessary to qualify its statement with the word "normally." We can only hope that diocesan and parish leaders will structure such freedom of choice for parents.

The Anointing of the Sick (127-128)

The Second Vatican Council stated that what had been called "Extreme Unction" may more fittingly be called the "Anointing of the Sick." It also stated that this "is not a sacrament for those only who are at the point of death" (Liturgy #73). The directory reflects these Council statements and the revised Rite of Anointing and Pastoral Care of the Sick in its emphasis on the need for the Church to care for the sick and to offer them the opportunity to celebrate this sacrament.

Catechesis for the Anointing of the Sick and their pastoral care are treated as a unity. This catechesis should consider "the meaning of sickness, healing, suffering, and death in the light of faith." It should encourage "the faithful to ask for the anointing and receive it with complete faith and devotion, not delaying its reception."

Members of the local parish are encouraged to visit the sick and express love and concern for them. The community should come to the sick to pray with them and to minister to their needs.

The directory also mentions some of those for whom this sacrament is intended: Those who are dangerously ill because of sickness or old age, patients undergoing surgery on account of dangerous illness, elderly persons who are in a weakened condition—even if they are not dangerously ill— and children who are seriously ill and have sufficient understanding to be comforted by its reception.

Catechists who are not familiar with the renewed understanding of this sacrament will themselves be in need of catechesis about it. Participation in the parish's pastoral care of the sick will best enable them to appreciate the Church's concern and love for its sick members.

Sacraments/Mysteries of Commitment

"Every Christian's ultimate commitment is to live and serve God revealed in Jesus Christ present in his Church." Christians live out this commitment in various ways. "Most do so in the context of marriage and family life, some by serving the faith community as ordained ministers" (129). This section considers Matrimony and Holy Orders as sacraments which celebrate such commitment.

The Sacrament of Matrimony (130-131)

Christian marriage is presented in the directory as "a loving covenant." The choice of the biblical theme of covenant to describe Christian marriage highlights its reciprocal character of self-giving and acceptance as well as its binding nature.

Catechesis for marriage begins in the home. Parents are the primary catechists of their children with respect to the value of Christian marriage. Young people of high school age need catechesis on Matrimony, married life, and Christian 'parenting.' Catechesis on Matrimony should be available at all stages of married life. Married couples, whenever possible, should be involved in this catechesis.

The directory states that marriage and conjugal love are by their nature ordained toward the begetting and education of children. It recognizes that the unitive goal of marriage is also important, and it includes a lengthy quotation from the Second Vatican Council:

> Marriage . . . is not instituted solely for procreation. Rather, its very nature as an unbreakable compact between persons, and the welfare of the children, both demand that the mutual love of the spouses, too, be embodied in a rightly ordered manner, that it grow and ripen. Therefore, marriage persists as a whole manner and communion of life, and maintains its value and indissolubility even when offspring are lacking —despite, rather often, the very intense deisre of the couple.

Catechesis for Matrimony includes instruction on the nature of the marriage relationship, the joys and problems of married life, and the responsibilities they will assume toward each other and their children. It "also includes a clear presentation of the Church's teaching concerning moral methods of regulating births, the evil of artificial birth control and of sterilization for that purpose, and the crime of abortion; it should stress the protection due to human life once conceived." Catechesis on Christian Marriage should be offered not only before marriage but throughout married life.

The section on Matrimony concludes with a paragraph urging the Christian community to be sensitive and helpful to those who have experienced divorce.

The Sacrament of Holy Orders (132-133)

Ordained ministry, that of bishops, priests and deacons, is a "sharing in the priestly saving action of Jesus Christ in a ministry of sanctifying, teaching, and building the Christian community."

Bishops participate in the fullness of the Sacrament of Orders. They are symbols of Christ present in the midst of his people "proclaiming the gospel and preaching the faith to all who believe."

Priests build up the Church. They, like bishops and deacons, minister "by proclaiming the word; embodying the gospel in the community of believers; and leading the community in worship, healing its divisions and summoning its members to reconciliation."

Deacons are ordained to serve all people through the threefold ministry "of the word, of the liturgy and of charity."

Catechesis on Orders will encourage the members of the community to support and pray for these ministers. It will reflect on the significance of this ministry within the Church so that they all may share a common vision of the task of these ministers.

Prayer (140-145)

Although each liturgy is an experience of prayer there are also other forms of prayer. Some of these forms are treated in Part C of Chapter 6 in the directory.

This section begins with a description of prayer: "Prayer, for both individuals and communities, means a deepening awareness of covenanted relationship with God, coupled with the effort to live in total harmony with His will" (140). Prayer is both private and communal. All prayer is an attempt to respond to the Holy Spirit dwelling within us. Private prayer helps the individual enter into communal or public prayer, and communal prayer leads the individual to private prayer.

The section on prayer contains articles on the Liturgy of the Hours, formerly called the Divine Office (141), *para*liturgies or scriptural celebrations (142), devotions and other forms of prayer (143), the liturgical year (144), and catechesis for prayer (145).

Much of what is said in the directory about the place of prayer in catechesis is found in Chapter 8 on "Catechesis Toward Maturity of Faith." This will be discussed in Chapter 5 of this book.

The Liturgy of the Hours is presented as a prayer form which has scripture as its source, which transcends the needs or insights of individuals and expresses the worship of the community. This prayer is made up of psalms, canticles, readings, hymns, responsories and intercessory prayers. It harmonizes with the sermons and themes of the liturgical year. The directory notes that "it can be adapted for families, parish groups and special occasions." Leaders in the parish community are urged to provide opportunities for the parish community and especially catechists to participate in this prayer.

"Paraliturgies or scriptural celebrations are forms of prayer which appeal to many Catholics today." They are similar in form to the Liturgy of the Hours with hymns, readings, responses, and intercessory prayers. They differ from the Liturgy of the Hours in that they are not ordinarily unified into a pattern of daily prayer nor do they necessarily follow the liturgical year. They are flexible in structure and can be designed for special occasions.

The article on devotions recognizes the rich tradition of devotions in both the Eastern and Western Churches. It states that "it is difficult to imagine a strong Catholic spiritual life without devotion to particular mysteries or saints." Devotions, both private and public, should harmonize with the liturgy, be in some way derived from it, and lead people toward it. Some devotions referred to in the article are: Eucharistic devotions, devotion to the Sacred Heart, the Way of the Cross, the rosary and other Marian devotions, and some devotions celebrated in the Eastern Catholic Communities.

Biblical prayer is another form of prayer which is highly recommended. Also recommended are the great traditional prayers of the Church, which express the Church's faith and enable people to pray together as a community, should be known by all. These prayers are listed the Apostles' Creed, the Sign of the Cross, the Lord's Prayer, the Hail Mary, and the Glory Be to the Father (143). Article 176e adds the Acts of Faith, Hope, Charity and Contrition.

All catechesis is oriented to prayer and worship. Through catechesis people are led to recognize God's presence in their lives and to respond to Him in prayer. Catechesis promotes active participation in the liturgy, encourages reflection on God's word and provides opportunities for prayer.

Sacred Art and Sacramentals (146-147)

This final section in Chapter 6 is relatively brief. It recognizes the fine arts as "among the noblest products of human genius. Whatever art forms are used in divine worship should be worthy, becoming, and beautiful" (146).

Through catechesis people should be introduced to the religious art of the past. "Contemporary art is as suitable for the service of religious worship as the art of past ages, provided it expresses the reverence and honor which are due the sacred" (146).

Sacramentals are holy signs which resemble the sacraments. "They signify effects, particularly of a spiritual kind, which are obtained through the Church's intercession" (147). In introducing sacramentals, such as baptismal water and holy oils, catechists should point out their relationship to faith and their function as signs in the life of the community.

Study Questions on Liturgical Signs

1. What is the function of liturgy? From where does it spring? How is it different from private prayer?

2. Name some changes in the ritual expression of liturgy that you have experienced in your life. How do you feel about these? Do they call for more involvement on your part? Is this good?

3. How is the catechesis related to liturgy? What are the implications of this at the local level?

4. What is the relationship between symbol and sacrament?

5. The Rite of Christian Initiation of Adults is presented as both a norm and a model for all sacramental catechesis. What are the implications of this on the local level? How can the local parish provide small community experiences for its members as well as those who wish to become members?

6. Most people in the Catholic Church are baptized as infants, not because of their own faith, but because of the faith of their parents and the community. How can the local community help young parents grow in their own faith and support them in parenting?

7. What are some of the problems connected with the catechesis for Confirmation? How are they being worked through locally?

8. "The Eucharist is the center and heart of Christian life." What are some aspects of Eucharistic celebration which you think need re-emphasizing as it is celebrated at the local level?

9. What is the value of small group liturgies? What groups participate in them in your parish or at your school? Should the opportunity to celebrate liturgy in a small group be offered to more people? What are some of the obstacles to doing this? How can they be overcome?

10. By participating in the Sacrament of Reconciliation Christians express the continuing process of converion which is going on in their lives. What does it mean to experience the "continuing process of conversion?"

11. How can we best prepare children for the Sacrament of Reconciliation?

12. How is the Anointing of the Sick celebrated differently now than it was ten years ago? What are the advantages of this?

13. How can married people at the local level participate in catechesis of marriage for young adults as well as for the Sacrament of Holy Orders?

14. Many people are experiencing a hunger for prayer and appreciate praying in small groups. How can this be implemented at the local level?

Articles in the NCD that refer to the Liturgical Signs						
Preface	Chapter 1	Chapter 2	Chapter 3	Chapter 4	Chapter 5	Chapter 6
9	15	30	55	65	82	All
	23	31	59	70	93	of
	24	32	60	72	97	this
		33		73	99	Chapter
		36		74	104	
		41		78	105	
		42		79		
		44		81		
		45				

	Chapter 7	Chapter 8	Chapter 9	Chapter 10	Chapter 11
	154	177	209	225	264
		178	211	226	
		179	212	227	
		180	213	228	
		183	214	229	
		185	216	232	
		189	217	242	
		191	218	243	
		201		245	
				247	

IV
The Ecclesial Signs

The word "ecclesial" refers to the inner nature of the Church. It differs from "ecclesiastical" which refers to the external workings of the Church. The ecclesial signs of catechesis are grouped under two headings. They are: the doctrinal or creedal formulations of the Church and the witness of Christian living (45).

Doctrinal or creedal formulations are "expressions of the living tradition which, from the time of the apostles, have developed "in the Church with the help of the Holy Spirit" (45). Throughout the directory these are generally referred to as the message of catechesis.

The witness of Christian living refers to the total life of the Church, including its manner of worship and the service it renders. The Church's worship is treated as a separate liturgical sign in catechesis. The Church's nature as a community and the service this community offers are grouped as ecclesial signs. The ecclesial signs of catechesis can, therefore, be listed as community, message, and service.

Through these signs God is revealing Himself to

the world today. God communicates Himself "through the witness of the faithful and through the full life and teaching of the Church" (55).

In *To Teach as Jesus Did,* the pastoral message of the bishops of the United States, issued in 1973, the educational ministry of the Church was presented as "an integrated ministry embracing three interlocking dimensions: the message revealed by God (didache) which the Church proclaims; fellowship in the life of the Holy Spirit (koinonia); service to the Christian community and the entire human community (diakonia)" (14). This pastoral message was on the topic of Catholic education. *Sharing the Light of Faith* expands catechetical ministry beyond the educational and schooling model presented in the earlier message. The new and broader model presented in the directory is based on the Church as a community. It is an ecclesial model. It continues to present community, message, and service as three dimensions of catechesis, and it perceives them as ecclesial signs of revelation.

Community

The fact that the bishops of the United States initiated an open and in-depth consultation process for the writing of the directory is evidence of their own understanding of the nature of the Church. The fact that the recommendations received were carefully studied and that the document changed considerably because of this process is another indication of their ecclesiology in practice.

Possibly no chapter was so radically changed by

the consultation process as was chapter 4 on "The Church and Catechesis." The final writing presents a vision of the Church which reflects the way in which the Church in the United States sees itself. It reflects the tensions within the Church which were expressed in the consultation. And it reflects the theology of the Church presented in the Vatican II documents.

Much of what is said about the Church is found in chapter 4. But again, this chapter cannot be read in isolation from the rest of the directory, for the entire document is permeated with an ecclesiology.

In the beginning of this chapter the Church is called a "mystery of divine love" (63). The word "mystery" is often thought of as that which cannot be understood. When used to describe the Church the word means that which can always be more fully understood. As mystery the Church is "a kind of sacrament." Mystery and sacrament have the same meaning, as is readily seen in chapter 6 where the words are often joined together as one word.

The Church is a mystery which reflects the very mystery of God Himself. It is a sacrament or symbol of Christ's continued presence in the world (63, 97, 114). In the consultation process the description of the Church as a "kind of sacrament" or "the universal sacrament" pleased a great many respondents and displeased some others. Those who were unhappy with this image of the Church found this description ambiguous and in need of refining. They inquired whether this meant that there were now eight sacraments.

The description of the Church as sacrament appears in the first article of Vatican II's *Dogmatic*

Constitution on the Church. There the Council stated
that because of her relationship with Christ "the
Church is a kind of sacrament of intimate union
with God, and of the unity of all mankind, that is,
she is a sign and instrument of such union and
unity." In other articles of this same constitution the
Church is called "a visible sacrament" (9), "a universal sacrament" (48). In the *Decree on the Church's
Missionary Activity* she is called "the sacrament of
our salvation" (5).

The Church is a sacrament in that it signifies
the presence of the redeeming Christ in the world. It
is a visible sign of this invisible reality. The Church
does not always show forth this reality equally well.
It is not always a convincing sign of Christ's presence. Its nature as sign or sacrament of Christ is
most evident when its members are united with one
another and with God in love and holiness, when
they come together to confess their faith in Christ
and to celebrate what God has done for them in
Christ. Through catechesis the community is called
to be this sign more fully.

The directory notes that the nature and mission
of the Church as mystery/sacrament are best captured in biblical parables and images. The images
express truth about the nature of the Church, and
they also challenge the Church to fulfill its nature.

These images of the Church are presented in a
catechetical document so that catechists may have a
fuller vision of the nature of the community they are
trying to build up through their ministry. No single
image captures the fullness of the Church's nature.
Some images may be more appealing to or appropriate for particular catechetical groups. All images

call the community to be more faithful to its nature. Fostering community which is one of the primary tasks of catechesis calls for an understanding of the nature of the community being fostered.

The images of the Church presented in the directory are: the people of God, one body in Christ, the Church as servant, as sign of the kingdom, as a pilgrim Church, and as a hierarchical society. Underlying all these images is a recognition of the Church as a community (70). Christ is the source of this communal identity. The Church is a community which shares beliefs, experiences, ideals, and values. It is one in which all members accept responsibility for themselves and the common good. All of the images which are presented in the directory and summarized in the following pages presume the Church is both community and sacrament.

The Church as a community of believers is called the people of God (64). This people is a chosen people, a priestly people, a holy people called to proclaim the glorious works of God. All members of the Church share in Christ's priestly ministry. All are called to offer sacrifice and to proclaim God's power (93).

The Church as community is also one body in Christ (65). Today, Christ is present in the world through the Church. The Church celebrates and expresses its identity as Body of Christ when it celebrates the Eucharist. The Church and the Eucharist are called by the same name, the Body of Christ.

The community of the Church is a servant community (66). As Christ its Lord came not to be served but to serve, so the Church seeks to serve, to heal, and to reconcile as Christ did. The serving nature of the Church is more fully developed in chapter 8 on "Catechesis for Social Ministry."

The Church is a sign or symbol of the kingdom (67). To fulfill its nature as sign of the kingdom, "The Church on every level—most immediately on the parish level—must be committed to justice, love, and peace, to grace and holiness, truth and life, for these are the hallmarks of the kingdom of God" (67).

The Church as a community is a pilgrim Church (68). It is a Church on its way. It represents now the beginning of the kingdom, but it is a kingdom not yet fulfilled. At present it still bears the burden of its own sins, weakness and frailty. It struggles patiently and lovingly to overcome the afflictions and hardships it meets and to show forth more fully its nature as symbol of the Risen Lord.

The Church is also described by certain signs or marks which identify this community of faith. The section in chapter 4 on the traditional marks of the Church (72) treats these signs, one, holy, Catholic, and apostolic, in a dynamic way rather than in a static apologetic fashion. It recognizes that they are gifts given to the Church but they are gifts which the Church must always strive to realize more fully in her life. In this section a special ecumenical sensitivity is present.

The Church is one because she is called to unity and is a sign of unity. She is holy because the holiness engendered by the Spirit "is expressed in the lives of Christians who strive to grow in charity and help others to do the same." The Church is catholic because the Gospel can be carried to and integrated with all cultures. The Church is apostolic not only because she traces herself back to Christ and the apostles, but also because she is continuing in fidelity "to Christ's loving and saving work and message, to ministry and service inspired by the evangelical vision and teaching of the original apostles" (72).

Through catechesis the Church attempts to build up the community. Some ways in which it does this are: by emphasizing its nature as a mystery/sacrament; by reflecting on biblical images which present the Church's nature and mission; by presenting those common beliefs and experiences, ideals and values which are the basis of shared life and unity in the Catholic community (74).

Catechesis for community gives opportunity to reflect on the characteristics or marks of the Church. It encourages missionary ministry and it emphasizes the need for fidelity to Christ's preaching and mission. It fosters understanding and unity by accurately presenting the history and practices of differing Church traditions. It recognizes the unity and diversity that exist within the Church (74).

Building Community

Throughout the directory the Church is presented again and again as a community. Article 70 describes the call of Christians to community. It does so in theological terms without addressing in detail the problem which the Church faces today in forming and fostering community on the local parish level. This problem is discussed, though not thoroughly, in other places in the document. Earlier the directory notes that except in certain rural areas and ethnic neighborhoods "Church leaders can no longer take for granted a sense of community. Often they must instead work to develop and sustain it" (21).

Some factors in our modern society increase the difficulty of building community. The mobility of our people is one example that is given in the directory. Almost one person out of five moves annually. It takes time to build community, to share beliefs, experiences, ideals, values with a new group of people.

One of the hopeful signs in the Church today is the formation of small communities, like the *communidad de base* which is found in the Hispanic community. These small communities provide an atmosphere for more effective catechesis (9). The formation of such small communities ought obviously to be encouraged.

The directory also mentions catechesis to groups of adults who are members of professional, social, or educational groups who already form a kind of community. It recommends catechesis for people in "the 'caring' professions" such as doctors, nurses, social workers (196). Campus ministers are urged to serve the entire campus community including students, administrators, faculty and staff (243). Chaplains to professional groups, such as police and fire departments, are encouraged to respond to the catechetical needs of these people. When community already exists, Christian community can build upon it and can be fostered more readily.

The Christian family is recognized in the directory as a "domestic Church," a "Church in miniature" (226). Efforts in family catechesis build on this basic community. They bring members of the family together for communication, prayer, and service. In this way they build community and provide support for already existing communities.

The Message

Chapter 5 of the directory is essentially a modified version of the *Basic Teachings for Catholic Religious Education* issued by the bishops of the United States in January, 1973. The *Basic Teachings* relied heavily on Part II, Chapter 2 of the *General Catechetical Directory* in which the parallel section was entitled "The More Outstanding Elements of the Christian Message."

In the editing of *Basic Teachings* an attempt was made to rewrite the document in a more dynamic way and give it a stronger biblical tone. Some recommendations received through the consultation process were incorporated in order to update the presentation. For example, the section on the moral life was rewritten and some sections moved to chapter 7 on catechesis for social ministry. This was done in order to incorporate parts of the document *To Live in Christ Jesus,* a pastoral reflection on the moral life issued by the bishops in November, 1976, and the *Declaration on Certain Questions Concerning Sexual Ethics,* issued by the Sacred Congregation for the Doctrine of the Faith in December, 1975. The section on the sacraments was also rewritten and presented as a separate chapter in the national directory.

Chapter 5 cannot be isolated from what precedes and follows it. In this chapter no attempt is made to determine how or when the message is to be

presented in catechesis. Guidelines for such presentation are found throughout the directory. Although an attempt was made to rewrite this chapter
in a style compatible with the rest of the directory,
the results are not wholly satisfactory. The presentation of the message is still somewhat static and
obviously an insertion. Perhaps that is unavoidable
when a previously written text is incorporated into
an original document.

The directory is not a catechism and does not
attempt to treat all the "truths" and "practices" to
which Catholics adhere. It presents in chapter 5
what it calls the "principal elements" of the Christian Message, but other elements are found in chapter 3 on "Revelation, Faith and Catechesis," chapter
4 on "The Church and Catechesis," chapter 6 on
"Catechesis for a Worshiping Community," and
chapter 7 on "Catechesis for Social Ministry."

In the preface, the directory notes that "not all
parts of this document are of equal importance. The
teaching of the Church in regard to revelation and
the Christian message is to be held by all; the norms
or criteria identified in article 47 pertaining to all
catechesis must be observed" (7).

Article 47 states that catechesis should present
the Christian message in its entirety. In children's
programs the textbook series *as a whole* is to be
evaluated in this regard (229, 181, 12). The interre-
lationship of the single parts of the message should
be apparent in catechesis so that the message will be
seen as forming an organic whole. This means recognizing a certain hierarchy of truths.

These truths may be grouped under four basic

heads: the mystery of God the Father, the Son, and the Holy Spirit, Creator of all things; the mystery of Christ the incarnate Word, who was born of the Virgin Mary, and who suffered, died and rose for our salvation; the mystery of the Holy Spirit, who is present in the Church, sanctifying it and guiding it until the glorious coming of Christ, our Savior and Judge; and the mystery of the Church, which is Christ's Mystical Body, in which the Virgin Mary holds the pre-eminent place (47; GCD, 43).

According to the directory, to say that there is a hierarchy of truths does not mean that some truths are less a matter of faith than others. It means that some truths of faith have a higher priority than others because these other truths are based on and illumined by them (47).

The four basic mysteries on which all truths are based are the mystery of God, the mystery of Christ the incarnate Word, the mystery of the Holy Spirit, and the mystery of the Church. They illumine all elements of the message. In chapter 5, twenty-seven articles present a synthesis of the Christian message. These articles are listed under the following sub-headings: the mystery of one God, creation, Jesus Christ, the Holy Spirit, the Church, the sacraments, the life of grace, the moral life, Mary and the saints, and a section on death, judgment, and eternity.

The proclamation of this message in catechesis "must be carried out under the guidance of the magisterium of the Church, whose duty it is to safeguard the truth of the divine message, and to watch that the ministry of the word uses appropriate forms of speaking, and prudently considers the help which theological research and human sciences can give" (47).

Catechists are reminded that when they "are engaged in the teaching dimension of their ministry, they teach not in their own names, but in the name of the Church" (16). They must be sensitive to the distinction between faith and theologies. There is one faith, but there can be many theologies. Pluralism in theological expression of the faith, which is common today, is not new in the history of the Church.

> Theological reflection is integral to the Church's life and thought. In the past, the Church not only tolerated but encouraged a pluralism of theological tendencies, reflecting attempts to provide better explanations of themes and problems addressed under different aspects. Today the Church continues to encourage pluralism for pastoral and evangelical reasons, provided always that the pluralism in question contributes to a genuine enrichment of the doctrine of the faith and is in constant fidelity to it. Theological expression also takes into account different cultural, social, and even racial and ethnic contexts, while at the same time remaining faithful to the content of the Catholic faith as received and handed on by the magisterium of the Church (16).

Dogmatic formulas or the way in which the Church expresses its faith in words may change. The meaning of these dogmatic formulas remains true and constant even when it is expressed with greater clarity or when there is a development of doctrine. As the directory states, "Because they are expressed in the language of a particular time and place, however, these formulations sometimes give way to new ones, proposed and approved by the magisterium of the Church, which express the same meaning more clearly or completely" (59). Human language is limited, especially when it attempts to express transcendent mysteries. For this reason it is valid to distinguish between the truth itself and the language or words in which it is expressed (45).

To proclaim the message adequately the catechist needs to have a clear understanding of what is meant by the development of doctrine. This means:

> (1) that new and deeper insights into the meanings and applications of doctrines can occur; (2) that new terminology can emerge for the expression of doctrine; and (3) that, through its magisterium, the Church can define doctrines whose status as part of divine Revelation and the Church's tradition is, in the absence of such definition, not explicitly evident (60).

Catechists are also asked to note the historical character of Revelation. In catechesis "memory of the past, awareness of the present, and hope of the future ought to be evident" (60). As God revealed the truth about Himself gradually over the centuries, so now the Church uses a pedagogy reflective of its experience of God. While expressing the message in its entirety it does so gradually according to the circumstances, readiness, and ability of those being catechized (176). Catechesis is not limited to one methodology, but whatever the method the catechist is "responsible for choosing and creating conditions which will encourage people to seek and accept the Christian message and integrate it more fully in their living out of the faith" (176).

More will be said later about the catechetical imperative of adapting to the circumstances of the catechized. Here it is sufficient to point out the parallelism between God's gradual revelation to humanity through the centuries according to people's readiness, their life stages, their needs and circumstances, and the effective catechetical approach which is based on the same considerations.

Many passages relevant to the principal elements of the Christian message are found throughout the directory. The role which the life sciences have played in raising questions in bioethics is acknowledged with the mandate that an awareness of the intrinsic value of life be the criteria upon which decisions are made in problems of abortion, infanticide, the aged, the severely handicapped, etc. (19).

Catechesis in morality is an integral part of catechetical ministry. Such catechesis "includes the Church's moral teaching, showing clearly its relevance to both individual ethics and current public issues" (38). Moral catechesis also takes into account the stages through which individuals and communities grow in ability to make moral judgments and to act in a responsible Christian manner. In relation to moral judgment the directory presents a rather long article (190) on the process of conscience formation.

Chapter 5 of the directory, which presents the

principal elements of the Christian message, is a brief, abridged summary of the Church's teaching. It is recommended that catechists refer to the directory itself for any questions they may have about the message. To abridge what is already a summary of the message for this book would indeed be to risk giving an inadequate presentation of it.

Service or Social Ministry

The Church continues the mission of Jesus through three closely related ministries: the ministry of the Word, the ministry of worship, and the ministry of service (30). Catechesis is a form of the ministry of the word which calls the Church to service. It supports the Church's ministry of service in its efforts to achieve social justice in the world (32).

Probably the most distinctive feature of the directory for the Church in the United States is that it incorporates within it a chapter on social ministry. The *General Catechetical Directory* by way of contrast has no such chapter. Integrating social ministry with catechesis reflects both the history of the Church in this country, and the growing concern of the United States Catholics for social justice.

Before one word of the directory was written, four documents were chosen as basic to its preparation. Three of these documents, the *General Catechetical Directory, Basic Teachings,* and *To Teach as Jesus Did* have already been mentioned. The fourth document, *Justice in the World,* is a statement of the Second General Assembly of Bishops in Rome, 1971.

In this document the synod stated that "action

on behalf of justice and participation in the transformation of the world fully appear to us as a constitutive dimension of the preaching of the Gospel,
or, in other words, of the Church's mission for the
redemption of the human race and its liberation
from every oppressive situation." The synod recognized that social ministry is an essential part of the
Church's mission. According to that same document
action for justice is inspired by love. It is a response
to God's love.

As a constitutive dimension of the preaching of
the Gospel, motivation to social ministry, which is
ordinarily called "service" in the directory, is an essential component of catechesis. All catechesis
should lead to service and to a recognition of the
demand of the Gospel for social justice.

Chapter 7 in the directory, "Catechesis for Social Ministry," presents a brief exposition of the
Church's bases for social ministry, an overview of
the development of Catholic social teaching, and a
mention of some contemporary social issues which
are of particular concern to the United States. In
this one chapter it is obviously not possible to give
more than an abridged introduction to these topics.
The purpose of the chapter is to present a context for
explaining why call to service is a basic task of
catechesis. In order to perceive the full meaning of
the chapter, it needs to be read in conjunction with
the entire directory.

The directory states that service, or social
ministry, is an ecclesial sign in catechesis. "God continues to manifest Himself through the Holy Spirit
at work in the world and, especially in the Church"
(54). He communicates Himself through the witness

of the faithful (55). The witness of the faithful in social ministry is that through which the serving Christ is revealed to the world.

Concern for and ministry to the poor, disadvantaged, helpless, and hopeless are signs that the Church is a servant. Uniting in love and mutual respect people from every corner of the earth, every racial and ethnic background, all socioeconomic strata, the Church is a sign of our union with God and one another effected in Jesus Christ. Every Christian community, characterized by its stewardship, is meant to be a sign of that assembly of believers which will reach fulfillment in the heavenly kingdom (45).

The Church as servant has a mission to heal, to reconcile, to assist those who are in need (66).

The Foundations of Social Ministry

The foundations of Catholic social teaching are found in scripture, in the development of moral doctrine in the light of scripture, in the centuries-old tradition of social teaching and practice, and in efforts to work out the relationship of social ministry to the Church's overall mission. The Church's social teaching has also been enriched by the contributions of philosophers and thinkers of all ages (150).

The directory presents biblical passages from both the Old and New Testaments which illustrate the Church's call to social ministry. Most of the Old Testament references are from the books of the

prophets. These prophetic statements called the
community to care for orphans, widows, aliens,
debtors, the oppressed, all who are in need. The passages quoted encompass those services which we
have traditionally called the corporal works of
mercy. The article catalogues many acts of justice
and mercy. It does not develop these themes. They
are presented in order to illustrate that the demand
for social ministry is a significant theme in the Old
Testament (152).

Through the same process the scope of social
ministry as presented in the New Testament is described. In the New Testament "the scope of social
ministry is broadened and social teaching is refined
. . . especially in the example and words of Jesus"
(153).

The teaching of Jesus on justice and mercy, as it
is presented in the Gospel and reflected in some epistles, is described or quoted. Some examples of Jesus'
unconditional giving of self to and for others are
noted (154).

This section may seem unsatisfactory because it
is so brief and the scriptural themes are not developed. Some readers may wish that other or additional
references would have been used. Also, there is always some danger in using biblical quotations out of
context. The reader needs to remember that the purpose of this section is to remind catechists that the
social ministry of the Church is an essential dimension of the Gospel. In the context of a catechetical
directory a fuller presentation of scriptural themes
did not seem possible. However, because of the importance of the biblical sign in catechesis, a fuller
presentation might have been helpful.

Chapter 7 continues by pointing out that the
themes of social responsibility found in the Bible
have been studied and explained in Catholic social
teaching. The fundamental concept of this teaching
is the dignity of the human person (156). This dignity is secure only when the spiritual, psychological,
emotional, and bodily integrity of each person is re-
spected as a fundamental value.

Flowing directly from the dignity of persons are
certain rights and duties which safeguard and promote this dignity. These basic rights and duties belong to all human beings regardless of "intelligence,
background, contribution to society, race, sex, class,
vocation, or nationality" (157). Catechesis for social
ministry provides opportunity for the community to
reflect on the implications of these rights and duties
for daily Christian living, and motivates the
catechized to live lives committed to social ministry
or service.

Social Morality

Another critically important aspect of Catholic
social teaching is its emphasis on social morality.
Because human beings are social by nature,
societies are essential to human development. The
organization and functioning of these societies raise
vitally important moral issues. Through its social
teaching the Church provides norms of conscience
for judging social structures and institutional relationships (158). Applying these principles to diverse
and complex social situations is not a simple matter.
So all members of the Church are urged to study

Catholic social teaching and to seek solutions to the unresolved social problems that they face.

In considering the relationship of social ministry to the mission of the Church the directory notes that the Church's religious mission is the source of its activities in the political, economic, or social order. Two documents of Vatican II, *The Church* and *The Church in the Modern World* agree that "a rounded view of the Church requires an understanding both of its inner life and of its ministry of service to society" (160). The Synod of Bishops in 1971 further expanded this understanding of social ministry in their statement on *Justice in the World.*

"Action of behalf of justice is a significant criterion of the Church's fidelity to its mission" (160). If the Church is to speak to others about justice, as its mission demands, then it must itself be just. During the consultation which preceded the directory a significant number of respondents expressed concern about justice within the Church itself. They felt that the document neglected this aspect of social justice. In the final writing the directory states that the Church must "submit its own policies, programs, and manner of life to continuing review" (160). The Church's use of temporal possessions in the face of dehumanizing poverty throughout the world is given as an example of a place where review may be necessary. Discrimination within the Church because of race, sex, and age might well have been included.

The remaining articles in this Chapter 7 present a brief overview of the development of Catholic social teaching, a short analysis of major concepts which are basic for understanding the social dimension of morality, and a reflection on some contemporary problems facing society. The chapter concludes with fifteen guidelines for justice, mercy and peace.

To summarize the brief overview of the historical development of Catholic social teaching would be to abridge an already too brief survey. This condensed version in the directory was inserted in order to assist catechists by placing present day Catholic social teaching in an historical context, and to show that Social Ministry is as integral to Church teaching as dogma and liturgical practice.

The directory analyses of the major concepts basic to understanding the meaning of social morality considers social justice, the social consequences of sin, and the relationship of justice and charity. "Social justice is the concept by which one evaluates the organization and functioning of the political, economic, social, and cultural life of society" (165). It applies the Gospel command of love to and within social systems, structures and institutions. The sin of injustice or "social sin" is expressed in some of the structures of human communities. These structures "involve a systematic abuse of the rights of certain groups or individuals." One example of social sin given in the directory is institutionalized racial or ethnic segregation. "Responsibility for correcting a situation of social sin rests upon all who participate in the society in question." Justice is the foundation and fulfillment of charity. It is love's absolute minimum (165).

Contemporary society faces certain issues of social justice. These issues are indicative of the scope and content of catechesis. They are grouped in the directory under the headings of respect for human life, national problems, and international problems. The section on contemporary problems catalogues a variety of issues that are of particular concern to the United States. Because they are of concern these issues must be addressed in catechesis. While it is important to have them listed and recognized as issues related to social ministry, some catechists will undoubtedly wish that the problems were addressed more fully. *Sharing the Light of Faith* is, however, a directory, not a catechism. The chapter on social ministry is an effort to present principles and guidelines for catechesis. Since motivation to service is one of the tasks of catechesis the overview presented in chapter 7 should be helpful to catechists.

Catechesis for Service

As action on behalf of justice and transformation of the world are a constitutive dimension of the preaching of the Gospel, so they are essential elements in catechetical ministry. Catechesis supports the ministry of service (32). It "includes the Church's moral teaching, showing clearly its relevance to both individual ethics and current public issues" (38). One of the fundamental tasks of catechists is to motivate individuals and communities to serve others (213). Catechesis concerning justice, mercy and peace, which are actions through which the Church serves, should be part of the catechetical process (170).

This catechesis leads people to recognize that

"the root causes of social injustice, selfishness, and violence reside within the human person." Catechesis for social ministry calls for a renewal of heart. It explains the relationship of personal morality to social morality. It strives to awaken a critical sense which leads individuals and the community to reflect on the values of society and to assess the social structures and economic systems which shape human lives (170).

Catechesis calls the community to remember the great men and women of the Church who have throughout the ages given themselves to the ministry of service. It challenges the men, women, and children of today to give of themselves in social ministry. It seeks to move all people "to live justly, mercifully, and peacefully as individuals, to act as the leaven of the Gospel in family, school, work, social and civic life, and to work for appropriate social change" (170).

Catechesis for service never ends. It is a continuing process which concerns persons of every age level. Chapter 8 in the directory gives some specific suggestions as to how this catechesis can be carried out at different stages of growth. These will be commented on in the next chapter of this book.

One of the major contributions which the bishops of the United States have made through this directory is the manner in which they have integrated social ministry with catechesis. They have left no doubt in the minds of readers that catechesis must motivate to service. They have expanded greatly on what was presented in seminal form in the *General Catechetical Directory*.

The Church in Dialogue

Particularly because of the religious pluralism
which is characteristic of society in the United
States, a special effort was made throughout the
directory to be sensitive to ecumenical concerns.
This sensitivity is expressed not only in the chapter
on the Church, but in many other parts of the directory as well.

The catechetical guidelines for ecumenism (76)
note that all Christians are called to support and
encourage ecumenism. Through catechesis the unity
of Christians can be fostered in many ways. Among
these ways are:

> by clearly explaining Catholic doctrine in its
> entirety and working for the renewal of the
> Church and its members; by presenting infor-
> mation about other Christians honestly and ac-
> curately, avoiding words, judgments, and ac-
> tions which misrepresent their beliefs and prac-
> tices; by communicating the divine truths and
> values Catholics share with other Christians
> and promoting cooperation in projects for the
> common good. Ecumenical dialogue and com-
> mon prayer, especially public and private peti-
> tions for unity, are to be encouraged. Catecheti-
> cal textbooks should conform to the guidelines
> found here and in the *Directory for Ecumenism*
> according to the age and readiness of learners.

Much of what is said about our relations with other
churches has been taken from the *Decree on*

Ecumenism of Vatican II, or the *Directory Concerning Ecumenical Matters.*

More Jewish people live in the United States than in any other country of the world, including Israel. As our neighbors we need to "be especially sensitive to relationships with the Jewish people" (77). The directory lists two other specific reasons which call for such sensitivity. First, we share a common biblical heritage. Second, "the tragic, scandalous, centuries-long persecution of the Jewish people, including the terrible holocaust in Central Europe and active persecution up to this day, calls for the specific and direct repudiation of anti-Semitism in any form and for determination to resist anti-Semitism and its causes" (77).

Most Catholics in the United States probably know less about the Moslem tradition than they do about the religious beliefs of the Jews and other Christians, yet as the directory notes, we have many beliefs and moral practices in common with the Moslem people. It is expedient in a time when Americans are coming more and more into contact with people of the Middle East than in the past to learn something of the religious traditions which Christians share with the Jewish and Moslem people. The directory, like Vatican II in the *Declaration on Non-Christian Religions,* presents in capsule form some of these beliefs and practices (78).

The directory points out that the Church regards the positive and enriching aspects of other religions, particularly Hinduism and Buddhism with honor and reverence. Catechists should "present an accurate account of the essential elements of traditional non-Christian religious beliefs" as perceived by the adherents of those beliefs, "develop an appreciation of their insights and contributions to humanity, and promote joint projects in the cause of justice and peace" (79). The Church also seeks to share the good news of Christ with these people (79).

The Church recognizes its relationship with those persons who profess no religion at all (80). There are approximately 81 million people in the United States who are not formally affiliated with any religion (14). "Catholics must strive to understand those who profess no faith and to collaborate with all persons of good will in promoting the human values common to all" (80). The Church seeks to share its faith with these people through evangelization.

Study Questions for Ecclesial Signs

1. The ecclesial signs of catechesis are community, message, and service. In what way have you experienced these signs? Of the three signs, which have you experienced the least? As a member of the Church, what can you do to alleviate this?

2. *Sharing the Light of Faith* presents a catechetical model based on the Church as a community. What are the catechetical programs in your locale doing to foster community? When the programs are evaluated, how is the community dimension taken into consideration? A community involves both children and adults. How is the primary

community, the family, involved? Some feel that the community dimension of catechetical programs is the weakest element. Do you agree? If so, how can this be changed? What are some of the factors in society which militate against a sense of community? Though the forming of communities may be difficult, there is a basic drive in humanity that strives for social relationships. How can large parishes or schools contribute to the formation of small communities?

3. The directory encourages family catechesis as a way to support and enrich the basic community. What efforts can be made locally to promote family catechesis?

4. Chater 5 of the directory deals with the message dimension of catechesis. Stop for a moment and list the five most important aspects of the Christian message that you think should be part of catechesis. Compare these with the hierarchy of truths mentioned in the directory and quoted in this chapter (article 47). Where are they different? How are they the same? Have you said many of the same things but in different words? Was your list implied in what the directory said?

5. The directory confirms that there is one faith in the Church but many theologies. In other words, the faith in Jesus can be expressed in different ways. Can you give examples of this?

6. The concept of the development of the doctrine is quoted in this chapter (article 60). Why is it

important for the catechist to have some grasp of this concept?

7. Service is the third ecclesial sign of catechesis. Quoting from the document of the Roman Synod of 1971, *Justice in the World,* the directory cites that "action on the behalf of justice . . . (is) a constitutive dimension of the preaching of the Gospel. . . . " How is the service component of catechesis manifested in the parish or school with which you are most familiar? Do you feel this dimension is a constitutive component or is it something tacked onto existing programs? Do you feel that there should be more awareness of the need for social justice in the world? How can this come about? Is the service dimension truly considered an important element in evaluating catechetical programs?

8. The NCD keeps alive the ecumenical search for unity found in previous Church documents. Besides promoting ecumenism among Christians, it reminds us of the common heritage we share with Jews and Moslems, as well as the positive aspects found in Hinduism and Buddhism. How can ecumenism be fostered through catechetical programs?

9. Brainstorm about effective ways of incorporating the community, message, and service components in programs for adults.

Articles in the NCD that refer to Community						
Preface	Chapter 1	Chapter 2	Chapter 3	Chapter 4	Chapter 5	Chapter 6
1	14	30	54	All	92	114
9	21	33	55	of	93	115
	25	34	59	this	94	117
		37	60	Chapter	97	118
		41			104	119
						120
		43				131
		45				

	Chapter 7	Chapter 8	Chapter 9	Chapter 10	Chapter 11
	160	180	209	222	
	162	181	212	225	
	171	182	213	226	
		185	214	227	
		194	216	194	
		195		230	
			217	233	
			218		
			221		

Articles in the NCD that refer to the Message						
Preface	Chapter 1	Chapter 2	Chapter 3	Chapter 4	Chapter 5	Chapter 6
7	16	30	48	63	All	114
	19	33	49	64	of	115
	24	36	50	65	this	116
		38	51	66	Chapter	118
		41	52	67		120
		45	53	68		124
		47	54	69		127
			55	71		130
			58	72		132
			59	74		
			60			

	Chapter 7	Chapter 8	Chapter 9	Chapter 10	Chapter 11
	152	176			
	153	190			
	154				
	156				
	157				
	159				
	160				
	165				
	167				
	170				

Articles in the NCD that refer to Service or Social Ministry						
Preface	Chapter 1	Chapter 2	Chapter 3	Chapter 4	Chapter 5	Chapter 6
9	13	30 32 38 45		67 69 72 77 78 79	86 89 91 96 98 105	119 121 125 148

	Chapter 7	Chapter 8	Chapter 9	Chapter 10	Chapter 11
	All of this Chapter	180 185 189 189 194	210 213 216 218	228 229 230 233 234 242	

V
The Natural Signs

During the last decade much of the controversy over religious education in this country has focused on the pros and cons of what has been called "the experiential approach." Opponents of this approach condemn it as "naturalistic" and "non-intellectual." They say it neglects to give adequate doctrinal formation. Proponents justify the experiential approach by noting that this approach is concerned with the totality of life, including reflection; that in this approach God is acknowledged as present in the totality of life; and that reflection on our experiences, in the light of faith, is a mode of catechizing that responds to human needs and desires. It is a reflection on the natural sign of revelation.

The directory emphatically accepts and recommends the experiential approach in catechesis without necessarily accepting all that has been done in its name. It acknowledges that one of the contemporary problems in catechesis is that "today most children are catechized in a way which bears little resemblance to the ways in which their parents received religious instruction" (10). This way is ordinarily the experiential approach, and it is obvious

that all those who are involved in the ministry of
catechesis will have to explain this approach adequately to parents.

The directory notes that human experience is of
great importance in catechesis (176d). Experiential
learning "gives rise to concerns and questions, hopes
and anxieties, reflections and judgments, which increase one's desire to penetrate more deeply into
life's meaning" (176d). Experience increases the
intelligibility of the Christian message; it should
be interpreted in the light of revelation. "The
experiential approach is not easy, but it can be of
considerable value to catechesis" (176d).

What does the directory mean by the experiential approach, and what is the basis of its acceptance
in catechesis?

The Natural Signs

The directory is based on the theology of revelation articulated at Vatican II. In the *Dogmatic Constitution on Divine Revelation* we read the following
statements: "God, who through the Word creates all
things and keeps them in existence, gives men an
enduring witness to Himself in created realities" (3).
"God . . . can be known with certainty from created
reality by the light of human reason" (6).

In the directory "the word 'revelation' is used
. . . to refer to that divine public revelation which
dozed at the end of the apostolic age. The terms
'manifestation' and 'communication' are used for the
other modes by which God continues to make himself known and share himself with human beings

through his presence in the church and world" (50).

The directory notes that "This manifestation of God is available to all human beings, even in the present condition of the human race" (49). Revelation is God's communication of Himself as gift, a gift that human beings do not deserve, but which is still given as gift.

Jesus fulfilled God's revelation through his life, death, resurrection and sending of the Spirit. "He confirmed with divine testimony what revelation proclaimed: that God is with us to free us from the darkness of sin and death, and to raise us up to life eternal" (Vatican II, Rev. 4). The fullness of Jesus' revelation will never be surpassed.

There are other forms of revelation through which God manifests and communicates Himself through His presence in the Church and the world. One of these forms is called "God's self-manifestation through creation" (51). revelation." Some signs of God's self-communication are creation, human beings, and human cultures (51).

"God manifests Himself through creation . . . because it is 'spoken' by God, creation is a great symbol of Him" (51). Creation is a present revelation of God. It is a symbol and like all symbols it makes present the reality of that which it symbolizes. Through creation God can be known.

"Because human beings are created in God's image and likeness they are most capable of making God manifest in their lives" (51). They are also symbols or signs of God's self-manifestation. This manifestation of the divine in human life is more clearly perceptible as people more fully live in fidelity to the image of God in them. We grow in knowledge and understanding of God when we respond to Him as He communicates Himself through the events of daily life and the triumphs and tragedies of history (55).

"Human cultures also mirror divine attributes in various ways" (51). Through the religions of humanity one can come to recognize "a Supreme Divinity and a Supreme Father too" (51). As belief can be expressed in the visual arts, in poetry and literature, in music and architecture, in philosophy and scientific or technological achievements, so these can also be signs of God's presence to us (59).

Not only can God be known through creation, human beings, and human cultures, but "God continues to manifest Himself through the Holy Spirit at work in the world and, especially in the Church" (54). The Spirit's action makes believers sensitive to God's prompting in their hearts. God communicates Himself through the full life and teaching of the Church (55).

God revealed Himself most fully through His Son Jesus Christ. God's revelation of Himself through Christ, through scripture and tradition, through the life of the Church, especially through her liturgy, and through all of creation calls for response. This response of self-surrender is known as faith.

The experiential approach is based on the Church's understanding of God's self-manifestation in our lives today. It is founded on the belief that God is present to us in our daily lives, and that if we reflect on the experiences of our life (the natural signs), in the light of the biblical, ecclesial, and liturgical signs, we will be challenged to respond in faith.

The Forms of Catechesis

Catechesis takes many forms. There is a particular kind of catechesis for different age levels, as well as for different groups within each age category (39). Catechesis also varies in form according to the language, vocation, abilities, and geographical location of those being catechized (39). Every form of catechesis is "oriented in some way to the catechesis of adults, who are capable of a full response to God's word" (32).

The directory presents guidelines for different age levels according to the following groupings: infancy and early childhood (birth to age 5); childhood (ages 6-10); preadolescence and puberty (ages 10-13); adolescence; early adulthood; middle adulthood; and later adulthood. It also makes recommendations for catechesis for persons with special needs, for example, different cultural, racial, and ethnic groups (194), persons with handicapping conditions (195), and other persons with special needs (196).

In all forms of catechesis the directory insists that "sound catechesis also recognizes the circumstances—cultural, linguistic, etc.—of those being catechized" (47). In chapter 8 alone it repeats more than twelve times that catechesis must be adapted to the age, level and ability, understanding, circumstances of life, level of faith, spiritual, intellectual, emotional and physical development of the catechized (176e; 177; 180; 181,1,4,12,13; 190; 194; 195; 196; 200).

The continued repetition of the need for adaptation points out one of the basic problems in modern catechesis, especially the catechesis of children and those persons who are from minority groups. Adap-

tation to any group of people cannot be made
without knowledge of those people. "How do children
grow in faith?" is a very important catechetical
question. How does immaturity affect the perception
of religious truth? What vocabulary, language patterns, and literary forms can a child comprehend? If
faith grows and matures, if it admits of various degrees "both in acceptance of God's word and in the
ability to explain and apply it," what are some signs
of growth? Is anyone able to describe the various
degrees of the life of faith?

The directory states that "catechesis is not limited to one methodology" (176b). It notes that the
Church today uses a pedagogy "in which the message is presented in its entirety while also being
expressed according to the circumstances and ability
of those being catechized" (176a). Some common
methods currently used in catechesis are story-
telling, discussion, role-playing, lecture, and the use
of media. Whatever methodology is used, it employs
inductive and/or deductive approaches. And these
approaches also have to be adapted according to the
persons being catechized.

"The inductive approach proceeds from the sensible, visible, tangible experiences of the person, and
leads, with the help of the Holy Spirit, to more general conclusions and principles" (176c). The inductive approach begins with experiences. For example,
it may begin with a reflection on a special family
meal or, when circumstances permit, a meal itself.
Consideration and reflection on characteristics of
special meals, such as the people present, conversa-
tion, special food, the occasion, elements of celebration, may lead to a discovery of some of the characteristics of the Eucharist as meal.

"The deductive approach proceeds in the opposite manner, beginning with general principles, such as a commandment, whether from the decalogue or the Sermon on the Mount, and applying it to the real world of the person being catechized" (176c). In the religious education of most of today's parents, the deductive approach was used. Today, catechesis of most children uses the inductive approach.

Both the GCD and the NCD express preference for the inductive approach, which is a form of experiential learning. The GCD notes that "the method called inductive offers great advantages ... This method is in harmony with the economy of revelation and with one of the fundamental processes of the human spirit, one that comes to grasp intelligible realities through visible things, and also with the particular characteristics of knowledge of the faith, that is, a knowing through signs" (GCD 72).

Use of the inductive approach in catechesis does not exclude the use of the deductive. But the national directory points out that the deductive approach is most effective when it is preceded by the inductive (176c).

Building on sensible, visible, tangible experiences of the person, is not easy, as the directory notes. But it needs to be done. This means that catechists need to be helped to understand the relationship between the life of faith and human development, and also how people grow in their ability to recognize and respond to God's revelation.

This does not mean that every catechist needs to be a professional psychologist. "Still, theoretical instruction is necessary for helping the catechist to meet various situations appropriately, for avoiding an empirical form of teaching catechesis, for grasping the changes found in educational reports, and for directing future work correctly" (GCD, 112c). The GCD is quite practical in stating that this instruction of the catechist can take place during sessions in which she or he is being helped to prepare for her or his ministry. These insights ought, obviously, to be incorporated into the catechist guides which are part of published programs. "Manuals for catechists should take into account psychological and pedagogical insights, as well as suggestions about methods" (175).

The directory states quite clearly that catechesis of adults is the chief form of catechesis (188). It is the summit of the entire catechetical endeavor, and it stands at the center of the Church's catechetical mission. This does not imply a lessening in commitment to children (40). It is simply an acknowledgement that adults are those who have the maximum human freedom that is capable of free response to God's grace (188), and they need the ministry of catechesis to help them grow to mature faith.

What the directory recommends regarding the different forms of catechesis is found primarily in chapters 8 through 11. In the following pages we shall attempt to summarize the main points of these recommendations according to the groupings used in the directory.

Infancy and Early Childhood (Birth to Age 5)

The directory points out that this beginning stage of life is of critical importance to the growth

and development of the child. During this time
"foundations are laid which influence the ability to
accept self, relate to others, and respond effectively
to the environment. Upon these foundations rests
the formation of the basic human and Christian
personality—and so also one's human capacity for
relating to God" (177).

Parents are the first and foremost catechists of
their children. "They catechize informally but pow-
erfully by example and instruction" (212). This is
the main reason why catechetical programs for pre-
school children should be directed primarily to their
parents (177, 230). Such programs provide the parents with opportunities to deepen their faith and become more adept at helping their children grow in
faith (230).

The parish community should support and
encourage parents (25). It can assist them in their
role as catechists of their pre-school children by education for parenthood and by pre-natal and pre-
baptismal catechesis (177).

How do parents catechize their young children?
By example; by sharing their attitudes and values
with their children; by speaking to their children
"naturally and simply about God and their faith", by
praying with their children (177).

Catechetical programs for the pre-school children themselves may also be desirable (230), providing that they "allow three-to-five-year-olds to develop at their own pace, in ways suited to their age,
circumstances, and learning abilities" (177). These
programs build upon what is positive in the family.
They are "of particular importance for children who
lack certain opportunities at home, children in one-

parent families, and those whose parents do not spend much time with them, either because they both work outside the home or for some other reason" (177).

When a parish provides formal catechetical programs for pre-school children, groups should be small, and at least one adult should work with the children of each level. The staff of the program should be composed of parents and other adults, and should include persons with training in such areas as theology, scriptures, early childhood growth and development, and methodology (177). The presence or availability of such a staff is one way in which present programs may be evaluated.

Childhood (Ages 6-10) and Pre-Adolescence (Ages 10-13)

There is remarkable growth in the child between the ages of six and ten. The child's "self-acceptance, trust and personal freedom undergo significant changes, with acceptance of self coming to involve an awareness of specific talents (or their absence), unqualified trust of others giving way to a qualified trust which excludes some people and situations, and the expression of personal freedom being modified by recognition that other people, too, have rights and freedom" (178).

All of these statements describing childhood have two parts. The first part (i.e., unqualified trust) describes the beginning part of this stage of growth. The second part (i.e., qualified trust) describes the end of the period of growth. Not every child is at the same stage at the same time. Catechists will need to know children on a one-to-one basis in order to perceive, generally, their capacity and ability.

During this time "intellectual capacity gradually expands. Before, the world was viewed in very concrete terms drawn from direct personal experiences; now, the ability to form abstract ideas or concepts based on experience increases" (178). During this stage, "Certain prayer formulas become more intelligible. Stories like the parables take on deeper meaning. Practices like sharing and helping others make a great deal more sense. Memorization can be used very effectively, provided the child has a clear understanding of what is memorized and it is expressed in familiar language" (178).

In pre-adolescence important physical changes take place which have a direct bearing on how pre-adolescents perceive other people and relate to them. Young people at this stage become consciously aware of themselves as male or female and of others as sexual beings. "They need to accept themselves precisely as male or female and to acquire a whole new way of relating to others." This period is sometimes characterized by "some confusion, uncertainty, curiosity, awkwardness, and experimentation as young people try on different patterns of behavior while searching for their own unique identity" (179).

Pre-adolescence is also a time of increased responsibility and freedom. It is a time of increased intellectual ability. For this reason "topics like the nature of scripture, the Church, the sacraments and the reasons which underlie moral norms can be discussed in greater depth than before. Reading and lectures can be used more effectively. But the life of faith is still best presented through concrete experiences which afford the pre-adolescent opportunities to incorporate Christian values into his or her life" (179).

The directory offers guidelines to assist catechists in their ministry to children and youth. It notes that the most important task of such catechesis is to provide through the witness of adults, an environment in which young people can grow in faith. The catechist, "in order to understand children and youth and communicate with them . . . must listen to them with respect, be sensitive to their circumstances, and be aware of their current values" (181,1).

The catechist needs to respect the intrinsic dignity of all young persons and recognize that "they are important not only for what they will do in the future, but for what they are here and now—for their intrinsic value and their value in relation to the common good" (181,2).

Catechists should work and plan together so that children have some experience of acting together as a community (135, 229). The home is the immediate environment in which children experience community but as they grow "the support of the larger community becomes highly important to education in the faith, and its absence a more serious matter" (178). For pre-adolescents, efforts to develop a sense of community and of membership in the Church should continue (179).

Proclamation of the Christian message is another integral element in catechesis. Although catechesis begins with experience it does not stop there. The catechetical process includes reflection on experience in the light of scripture and tradition. This is done according to the age and capacity of the catechized.

The directory notes that textbooks, which are ordinarily used as the basic curriculum in the catechesis of children and adolescents, should "present the authentic and complete message of Christ and His Church, adapted to the capacity of the learners, with balanced emphasis proportionate to the importance of particular truth" (264). It is the curriculum as a whole, that is, all six or eight textbooks of the program, as well as other components such as materials for parents that are to be evaluated to determine if its content is comprehensive enough (229; 181,12).

Through catechesis for social justice and service children should be encouraged to know and respect other cultural, racial, and ethnic groups. Although the concept of service has "limited application" on the elementary level (229), "service oriented class projects can be introduced in the intermediate grades" (229). By junior high service projects such as visiting the aged or shut-ins, assisting catechists who teach handicapped children, and working with community action programs should be part of the catechetical program (229, 228). "Catechesis for justice, mercy and peace is a continuing process which concerns every person and every age." It should be an integral part of all parish catechetical programs (170).

All catechesis should lead to prayer. Ideally children first experience prayer in the home. As they mature they ought to be introduced to those common

prayers of the Church which are expressions of the
Church's faith. Sharing common prayers enables
Christians to pray together. Catechesis on the meaning and symbols of sacramental celebrations enables
children, according to their capacity, to enter more
fully into the celebration. "Children often cannot
participate fully in adult liturgies because they do
not understand the words and symbols used or understand them only imperfectly" (135). Therefore,
they should be given opportunities to celebrate the
Eucharist together. "Family participation in Masses
for children is encouraged on occasion in order to
encourage family unity" (135).

Preparation of children for First Communion
and their initial experience of the Sacrament of Reconciliation has been presented in chapter 3.
Catechesis for these sacraments does not end with
their first reception. Continued catechesis on the
Eucharist and Reconciliation should be part of children's catechesis each year.

"The vital influence of parents on the social and
religious development of their children must be
more widely recognized" (25). It is parents who are
the "first and foremost" catechists of their children.
Ideally, parents catechize their children directly
(226), but parish catechetical programs for children
are provided in order to help parents in their
catechetical role.

Programs for parents should focus on the task of
the parents in relation to particular moments or issues in the child's religious life, such as sacramental
preparation and moral development. They also seek
to familiarize parents with the stages in children's
growth and the relevance these have for catechesis

(212). All materials published for children should include manuals or developed notes for parents (264).

Family catechesis is highly recommended in the directory (197, 226). Family-centered catechetical programs bring the members of the family together to learn, experience, and celebrate some aspect of Catholic belief or living. They help parents carry out their responsibilities in and to the Church's catechetical mission. Such programs build community within the family, encourage parents and children to serve one another, enable them to share the meaning of their Christian faith, and provide opportunity for family prayer (226).

Throughout the directory Catholic schools are recognized as an integral part of the parish's total catechetical program. The Catholic school contributes to the parish upon which it depends. Its catechetical program complements the total program of the parish. Catholic schools are recognized as unique expressions of the Church's effort to achieve the purposes of Catholic education among the young. "Its nature as a Christian educational community, the scope of its teaching, and the effort to integrate all learning with faith distinguish the Catholic school from other forms of the Church's educational ministry to youth and give it special impact" (232).

All that is said about the catechesis of children and youth applies to the Catholic school. Building community, proclaiming the message, motivating to service, and leading to prayer ought to be explicit goals of the contemporary Catholic school.

Catholic schools are to give witness to the

Church's care for the needy, the disadvantaged, and those "who are strangers to the gift of faith" (233). They have a special role in the Church of giving witness and fostering evangelization.

Adolescence

The directory does not give a specific age bracket for adolescence but points out that "different cultural, racial, and ethnic groups have their own standards for determining the length of time between puberty and adulthood" (180). For this reason there is some overlapping between the guidelines given for pre-adolescents and early adulthood with those given for adolescents. In fact, article 181 combines the guidelines for children with those for adolescents. In this section we shall consider what the directory says about adolescents or ministry to youth as distinguished from early adulthood.

Youth catechesis is described as being most effective within a total youth ministry. It requires the collaboration of many people with different kinds of expertise. "It is *to* youth in that it seeks to respond to adolescents' unique needs. It is *with* youth in that it is shared. It is *by* youth in that they participate in directing it. It is *for* youth in that it attempts to interpret the concerns of youth and be an advocate for them" (228).

Ministry to youth should include a variety of approaches including social, recreational, and apostolic programs as well as retreats and other spiritual development activities. It "includes catechetical activities in which the message is proclaimed, community is fostered, service is offered, and worship is celebrated" (228).

No single model of catechesis for youth is proposed. Decisions should be made on the local level as to whether such programs should be "parish or home-centered, whether they should have a formal 'classroom' or informal 'group' format, whether they should be scheduled weekly over an extended period of time or concentrated in a shorter time span, or whether some particular mixture of formats and schedules should be employed" (228). When programs are planned for young people, they themselves should be involved in the planning.

Whatever programs are planned should be based on an understanding of the adolescent stage of growth. Adolescence is described as a time when youth are searching for personal identity. This search, which often includes self-doubt, may be expressed externally by symptoms of boredom, frustration, sharp changes in mood, withdrawal, rebelliousness, apathy toward religion.

Because adolescents are seeking independence they sometimes "reject, or seem to reject, laws and rules which they regard as arbitrary, external restrictions on their personal freedom. Many substitute a kind of inner law or norm of behavior based on personal ideals" (180). They are increasingly critical of real or imagined imperfections in the Church. For this reason the faithful witness of the adult community is extremely important.

"Adolescents also commonly manifest increasing spiritual insight into themselves, other people, and life in general" (180). They become more intellectually competent and need more intellectual stimulation and growth. They begin to make vocational choices. They develop a greater capacity for authentic love of others. They have an increasing ability to respond with a mature faith.

All of these characteristics must be considered when planning youth catechesis. The strong influence of peers and the need for the Christian witness of adults are natural bases for the building of community. The community dimension of catechesis can be fostered in small groups within which relationships can develop. It can be strengthened in weekend prayer experiences and retreat experiences.

Community is also fostered through recognition of the Christian demands of social justice and service. Service opportunities of many different kinds should be part of catechetical programs for youth (228). These experiences help develop lasting motivation for service to others. Catechesis should foster in these young people a social conscience sensitive to the needs of all (232).

Recognition of the adolescent's increased intellectual ability enables a fuller proclamation of the Christian message. At this time "it is possible to make more use of systematic, formal methods of instruction and study. However, deductive reasoning and methodology are more effective when preceded by induction" (181, 10). Catechesis for youth should provide opportunities for specific experiences through which young people can apply the message of the Gospel and live out their faith (181, 10).

The directory recommends that the study of scripture, the Church, the sacraments, and morality be part of the overall program for youth. "Multiyear programs are best evaluated in their totality" (181,

12). In a comprehensive ministerial program to youth this instruction will flow from and lead to service, liturgy and community (228).

In youth catechesis private prayer will be presented as a mode of individual reflection and communication with God. Because "ritualized prayer often loses its attraction" at this time (180), catechesis on the symbols and symbolic actions of the Church's worship is imperative. Young people should be given opportunity to prepare and plan Masses which reflect their faith and their feelings (136). Catechesis should be provided on the way in which the Church celebrates its union with Christ in the Eucharist, and of liturgy's intimate relationship to life, faith, doctrine, and the Church. "Young people who see no point to prayer and meditation should be introduced—or reintroduced—to the idea that it is personal communication with Jesus and, through and in Him, with the Father" (180).

In youth catechesis a variety of activities, such as "field trips, meaningful social action, weekend retreats and programs, group dynamics of a sound and tested nature, simulation games, audio-visuals, and similar techniques can be very helpful. Constructive interaction and personal involvement are extremely important, and are present in Gospel-based value clarification, group discussions, programs for the development of communication skills, and group prayer" (181, 10).

Adults

At one point in the consultation process the issue of greatest concern in the recommendations on adult catechesis was whether or not the Church is truly committed to this ministry. The GCD had stated that "catechesis for adults, since it deals with persons who are capable of an adherence that is fully responsible, must be considered the chief form of catechesis" (19). The bishops of the United States in their pastoral message *To Teach As Jesus Did* stated that "the continuing education of adults is situated not at the periphery of the Church's educational mission but at its center" (43). Still, the question as to whether the Church is really committed to this ministry was repeatedly raised. Comments implied that little had been done to make adult catechesis a priority.

The fact that this question arose at all is evidence of the growing consciousness within the Church of the need for the catechesis of adults. These earlier Church documents clearly brought this need to mind as a priority within the Church. The directory expands greatly on these past statements and calls for the catechesis of adults of every age in very specific ways.

The directory notes that one of the principal reasons for regarding the catechesis of adults as the chief form of catechesis is that "maximum human freedom only comes with the self-possession and responsibility of adulthood" (188). It is the adult who is most fully free to respond to God's revelation of Himself. Challenging and calling the adult to ever fuller response, or growth in faith, is the principal goal of adult catechesis (25, ftnte 14).

The directory analyzes the growth of the adult as it did the growth of children and adolescents. It points out that there are three distinct stages of adulthood: early adulthood (approximately between the ages of 18 and 35), middle adulthood, and later adulthood. Each stage has its own special and unique characteristics. At each stage adults are in need and have a right to catechesis which responds to these characteristics.

Those persons considered as young adults belong to many different groups and these groups have overlapping membership. They may be high school students, members of the military, college, university and technical school students, blue collar workers and professionals, or unemployed men and women. They may be members of particular cultural, racial, or ethnic groups. They are single, married with children, married without children, unmarried with children, separated, divorced, or widowed. Some may have physical handicaps, be emotionally disturbed or mentally retarded. Each individual and group has its own needs and a variety of catechetical approaches are needed to respond to these needs (181).

During the time of early adulthood long-term choices and decisions are made concerning vocations, careers, and religious affiliation. Through catechesis the Church seeks to help these young persons reflect on the meaning of their lives and make these decisions in the light of revelation (183).

This is a time when many young people "are engaged in an intense search for spirituality and values" (227). Some are alienated from the institutional Church and within this group are some of those "the most likely to sever contact with organized religion" (182). The Church needs to be present to them, to seek them out, to listen to them and to share the good news with them.

The concept of middle adulthood is a relatively

new concept. By middle age the high goals, self-confidence, optimism, and enthusiasm of youth have been tempered. Limitations and possibilities have become more apparent. Both success and failure in life have been met.

In middle age persons can exercise a more truly personal freedom. Positive acceptance of the realities of limitations and possibilities means moving to a new stage of maturity which can be the basis for deepening of faith. Catechesis can help these adults live out their life decisions. It can prepare them for difficult moments of life and assist them through these moments (183).

The directory presents many guidelines for the catechesis of these adults (185). It notes that all effective planning for catechetical ministry is person-centered (221), and that Church-sponsored programs for adults should respond to the expressed needs of the participants (227). This catechesis "should confront people's real questions and problems honestly and openly. As far as possible, they should offer positive reinforcements and rewards; the learning environment should be attractive and comfortable; adults should be encouraged to realize their potential for becoming religiously mature—or more mature—persons" (189). Adults should play a central role in their own catechesis. They should identify their needs, participate in planning ways to meet them, and should take part in the evaluation of programs and activities.

For young adults in particular, catechesis must be developed and conducted in ways which emphasize self-direction, dialogue, and mutual responsibility. These programs should include psychologi-

cal and sociological matters considered in the light
of faith, questions of faith and moral issues, and
similar matters pertaining to human experience
(227).

Reflection on experience in the light of faith is
an effective learning process not only for children
but also for adults. Through this process adults may
be helped to recognize God's action in their lives and
to live in a more fully Christian way. "Where appropriate experiences have not been part of a person's
life, the catechetical process attempts to provide
them, to the extent possible" (185). This can be done
through the use of discussion techniques, especially
in small groups, and the cultivation of communication skills.

Catechesis of adults should always reflect the
four inter-related purposes of catechesis: to proclaim
the mysteries of faith; to foster community; to
encourage worship and prayer; and to motivate service to others (227).

The catechesis of adults proclaims the mysteries
of faith through reflection and study of scripture,
tradition, liturgy, theology, morality, and the
Church's teaching authority and life. A knowledge
of Church history helps to place events in proper
perspective. Proclaiming the mysteries also includes
reflection and dialogue on the Church itself, "its
missionary nature, its role as sign or sacrament of
Christ's presence in the world, its ecumenical commitment, and its mandate to communicate the whole
truth of Christ to persons in all times" (185a).

Catechesis fosters community. The directory
notes that one of the positive developments in
catechesis today is the formation of small Christian

communities which provide an atmosphere or environment for effective catechesis (9). These small communities already exist in the Church. Catechesis builds on already existing communities and seeks to strengthen them. Where community does not exist or is weak, catechesis provides opportunity to develop it.

The catechesis of adults encourages worship and prayer. It does this by providing opportunity for community and individual prayer in retreats, week-end encounters, prayer days, times for silent prayer, and through liturgies celebrated by the catechetical communities. Adults should be introduced, or reintroduced, to the psalms, canticles, readings, hymns, responsories, and intercessory prayers which are part of the Church's life and their heritage. Catechesis of adults includes reflection on the symbols and rituals of the sacramental mysteries so that they may participate more fully in them.

Consideration of the demands of social justice is another integral component of adult catechetical programs (170). Catechesis for justice, mercy, and peace seeks to bring people to recognize their individual and collective obligations to strive to overcome the grave injustices in the world. It attempts to awaken in men and women a critical sense which leads them to reflect on society and its values and to assess, in the light of the Gospel, the social structures and economic systems which shape human lives. According to the directory adult catechesis on social justice and the biblical concept of stewardship is needed and should be given priority (170).

A variety of approaches including reading, lectures, workshops, seminars, the use of the media, the Catholic press and other publications, retreats, prayer meetings, "in fact, all methods available to sound secular education" (185), may be used in adult catechesis.

Catechesis is a process which ideally goes on throughout life. It is to be offered to all members of the Church. If in the immediate past the Church has neglected some persons or groups, now that deficiency should be remedied (196).

Later Adulthood

The directory has several articles on the importance of providing catechesis for the elderly (186, 187, 202). It notes that, generally speaking, pastoral ministry has paid too little attention to the elderly. In particular catechesis has seldom responded to the needs of this age group (186). Yet catechesis is meant to help at each stage of human development (174), including later adulthood.

Although no specific age is given for this stage of life, in one place the directory refers to persons who are 65 or older. Catechesis seeks to offer these people "physical, emotional, intellectual, and spiritual support so that they can make fruitful use of leisure time, understand and accept the increasing limitation imposed by age, and grow in faith even as they grow in years" (187).

Elderly people can make significant contributions to the entire community through their work and witness. They can, themselves, provide some of the most effective catechesis for the aged. For this reason they should be prepared to participate in

catechetical ministry and to plan and direct programs for their own groups.

Pastoral ministers should know how many elderly people are living in the parish and the diocese.
Those who are living in nursing homes should be
ministered to by catechists prepared with appropriate experiences to offer this service (244).

Study Questions for Natural Signs

1. When someone speaks of the "experiential
approach in catechesis," to what is one referring?
Cite examples.

2. Why is human experience an important basis
for catechesis? Name some faith experiences in your
own life. Upon what human experiences were they
based?

3. Name some aspects of faith which you have
found expressed in the visual arts. In poetry and
literature. In music and architecture. In philosophy
and scientific or technological achievements.

4. The directory says that every form of
catechesis is "oriented to the catechesis of adults,
who are capable of a full response to God's word."
The list which follows suggests a number of topics
upon which catechesis for adults could be planned.
Rank these according to the needs you perceive.
1=most needed; 19=least needed.

—— Parenting
—— Communication with teens

—— Marriage enrichment
—— Scripture studies
—— How to prepare my child for the Sacrament of Reconciliation
—— How to cope with my mid-life crisis
—— How to pray
—— How to enjoy growing old
—— What to do when the last child is in school
—— How to be a happy single
—— New morality
—— Family education
—— Prayer
—— Other Religions
—— Quality of Life
—— Peace and War
—— Wealth and Poverty
—— Human Rights
—— Human Dignity

What steps can you take to begin to meet the needs assessed above?

5. An essential principle to be considered in catechesis is the adaptation of the program to the age, level and ability, understanding, circumstances of life, level of faith, spiritual, intellectual, emotional and physical development of the catechized. The NCD continually repeats this. How is this principle being implemented in the programs with which you are most familiar? What aspects of the program are weak in this adaptation? Have you seen evidence of programs that are weak because they did not meet the needs of those to be catechized, whether they be children or adults?

6. What are some important points to be kept in mind when catechizing?
   A. Young children (birth-5)
   B. Children from 6-10
   C. Children 10-13
   D. Adolescents
   E. Young adults
   F. Families
   G. Adults in their middle years
   H. Divorced and widowed
   I. Senior citizens

7. How can catechesis in each one of the areas mentioned above foster social justice?

Articles in the NCD that refer to the Natural Signs						
Preface	Chapter 1	Chapter 2	Chapter 3	Chapter 4	Chapter 5	Chapter 6
9	26	32	49	72	84	114
10	27	33	51	80	85	117
	29	34	53		86	128
		35	54		92	135
		38	55		95	
		39	59		102	
		41	60		104	
		42				
		43				
		46				
		47				

	Chapter 7	Chapter 8	Chapter 9	Chapter 10	Chapter 11	
	156	All	221	227	264	
	158	of		228		
	170	Chapter		229		
		8				

VI
The Catechist

The majority of Catholics ordinarily do not read Church documents. They read about them in newspapers or magazines or they hear about them from leaders in the Catholic community. When over 40,000 copies of the *General Catechetical Directory* were purchased, it was considered a surprising sale. This large circulation was even more unusual since the GCD was intended for a limited audience, namely, "bishops, conferences of bishops, and in general all who under their leadership and direction have responsibility in the catechetical field" (GCD, Foreword). The wide distribution of that document reflected the concern and interest that Catholics have in this ministry, particularly as it affects their children.

The NCD was prepared "particularly for those responsible for catechesis in the United States" (6). This is the same audience for whom the GCD was written. But the NCD also hopes to reach a wider audience and benefit many others, including parents and catechists.

Catechists on every level will find the directory supportive of them. As the GCD recognized that the catechist is of prime importance in catechesis (GCD 71), so does this directory acknowledge that it is the catechists themselves, more than their methods and tools, upon whom the success of catechesis depends (294).

It also recognizes that there are limits to what catechists can do. They are responsible for choosing and creating suitable conditions in which the message can be proclaimed, community can be fostered, people will be led to prayer and social ministry (213). "This is the point to which the action of the catechist extends—and there it stops" (GCD 71). Since faith is a gift, adherence to God in faith on the part of those being catechized "is a fruit of grace and freedom, and does not ultimately depend on the catechist" (GCD, 71; NCD, 213). Catechists need to recognize that "another, mysterious, uniquely powerful action is taking place, the work of the Holy Spirit in each person, in the Church, and in the world" (203). St. Paul understood the limits of Christian ministry when he wrote the Corinthians:

Who is Apollo? And who is Paul? Simply ministers through whom you became believers, each of them doing what the Lord assigned him. I planted the seed and Apollo watered it, but God made it grow. This means that neither he who plants nor he who waters is of any special account, only God who gives the growth (1 Cor. 3, 5-7).

It Is the Community That Catechizes

Who can be a catechist? The directory notes that parents are catechists and that many persons in the parish volunteer to catechize. For all catechists the fundamental tasks are the same: "to proclaim Christ's message, to participate in efforts to develop community, to lead people to worship and prayer and to motivate them to serve others" (213). All have the same tasks. Do all need the same skills and competencies?

Sprinkled throughout the directory are a great number of "essential" competencies which are expected of catechists. Unless these required competencies and skills are read with the perspective of the directory, namely, that it is the community which catechizes, catechists might unnecessarily be frightened from participating in this ministry. Reading from the directory a partial listing of the competencies and skills expected of the catechists makes it quite clear that it is the Church as community which catechizes. For example, according to the directory, catechists should:

be sensitive to the difference between faith and theology (16);

recognize the unequal value of various theological systems (16);

have an awareness of the positive and negative aspects of contemporary cultural and religious factors confronting society (29);

be able to use examples from daily life, the arts, and the sciences to draw out the meaning of God's revelation and show its relevance for contemporary life (60, ii, a);

have a clear understanding of what is meant by the development of doctrine (60, ii, c);

foster understanding and unity among Catholics by accurately presenting the history and practices of each Church tradition in the context of the Universal Church (74, g);

present an accurate account of the essential elements of traditional non-Christian beliefs, such as Hinduism and Buddhism, as these beliefs are perceived by adherents of these religions (79);

experience the richness and beauty of the Liturgy of the Hours (141);

be familiar with sacramental theology and the principles of liturgical celebration (145);

familiarize themselves with liturgical law and official guidelines relating to liturgy (146);

be able to discuss the relationship of sacramentals to faith and their function in the Church and in the lives of individuals (147);

be critical in their approach to the behavioral sciences (175);

recognize the value of the inductive approach and know when the deductive approach may be used with it (176);

recognize the value of the experiential approach

in catechesis and be able to use it (176);

have a suitable preparation so they can incorporate catechesis in sexuality into their program (191);

have a solid grasp of Catholic doctrine and worship (211);

have an understanding of how people grow and mature and of how persons of different ages and circumstances grow (211);

know and be able to use the results of research (223);

have some understanding of the implications of media for their work (252);

investigate the possibility of applying for broadcast air time in order to present programs (256);

be informed participants in the development of cable television (258);

provide the Catholic press with news releases and photographs (259);

cooperate with the Catholic press as planners, consultants, and writers (259);

be prepared to respond to press inquiries and to spend time, when necessary, discussing questions and issues with journalists (260);

be trained in the use of media. Training will
cover such things as the "language" of film
and television and the characteristics of different media (265).

Not many members of the Catholic community
could offer to catechize if all of these competencies
were required of each of them. The listing graphi-
cally illustrates an essential truth of which all
catechists need to be aware: it is the community
which catechizes.

Within the community are many gifted members. Each member does not possess the same gifts
that other members do. The Holy Spirit acts within
the whole Church distributing His gifts according to
His desire. Each member is gifted. The gifts of each
member are needed. Together, as a community the
Church catechizes.

Sometimes individual Christians hesitate to respond to the call to be catechists. They desire to do
so, but feel inadequately prepared. Leaders within
the diocese and parish are encouraged to discern the
giftedness of the members and call them to exercise
their responsibility as members of the community
which catechizes. Each member exercises responsibility in a different way, and each member brings
unique gifts to the catechizing community. All work
together to fulfill the mission of the whole Church.

The directory notes that the bishop is the chief
catechist in the diocese (218). It also states that "the
bishop does not work alone. He is assisted by parents, catechists, directors and coordinators, religious, deacons, and priests" (218).

The bishop is responsible for choosing qualified

men and women as leaders for the catechetical ministry in the diocese. He is to ensure that catechists are adequately prepared for their ministry by providing opportunity for continuing education for all who exercise catechetical roles. He is also to be, as the directory states, "mindful of his own need for continuing education" (218). If the bishop, as chief catechist, is called to recognize his own need for continuing education, so also is every other person who acts as a catechist.

The bishop carries out his responsibility in a personal way by devoting himself to the work of the Gospel (218), and through diocesan structures, such as the diocesan pastoral council, the diocesan catechetical/education board, and the diocesan catechetical office (238). The persons who staff this office "should have previous catechetical experience in parishes or schools, as well as formation comparable to that required of parish directors, coordinators, and teachers in Catholic schools" (218).

The members of the diocesan staff serve the diocesan Church in many ways. They are to "encourage and motivate catechists on every level by visits, in-service training, newsletters, diocesan institutes, etc." (218,1). They are to "provide prior training and continuing education for catechists by establishing permanent centers for catechetical training or cooperating with Catholic colleges or universities in setting up such programs" (218,6).

Catholic universities are urged to provide a variety of programs for persons who desire to prepare for professional careers in catechetical ministry (242,a). Catholic colleges are encouraged to offer undergraduate degrees in catechetics and theology "both for those who wish to pursue graduate studies and become fulltime catechetical workers and for those who may assume other leadership roles in the Church" (242,b). They are also asked to cooperate with diocesan offices and neighboring parishes in determining local needs and providing in-service training for catechists. All who are involved in catechesis, parents (212), parish catechists (214), directors and coordinators of religious education (214), school principals (215), permanent deacons (216), and priests (219), are urged to continually study and update themselves in a variety of ways so that they may more adequately exercise their catechetical ministry.

No catechist works alone. All work together as a community. Individual catechists need to experience community, not only the community of the parish as a whole, but also the community of those called to catechize for this community. Parishes and dioceses are encouraged to cultivate "a sense of community among the catechists during the entire formation process" (213,7). Catechists should have opportunities "to experience this unity through frequent participation in the celebration of the Eucharist with other catechists and with those being catechized" (209). "Community is formed in many ways. Beginning with acceptance of individual strengths and weaknesses, it progresses to relationships based on shared goals and values. It grows through discussion, recreation, cooperation on projects and the like" (209).

All members of the community of believers are called to share in the ministry of catechesis by being witnesses to the faith (204). Some members are called to fulfill specific catechetical roles for a time.

During the time when these members are being prepared for this role, leaders within the parish, region, or diocese can enable them to strengthen or acquire the competencies and skills needed for their particular ministry.

Catechists Are an Ecclesial Sign

One ecclesial sign of catechesis is "the witness of Christian living" (45). This ecclesial sign includes the total life of the believing community. The Church itself is a symbol or sacrament of Christ.

As a catechizing community the Church symbolizes Christ's love for his followers. Those who are called to fulfill particular catechetical roles in this Church are called to make present, through their lives, the loving concern of Christ

The directory describes some ideal qualities of catechists. It acknowledges that these are "ideal" qualities, presented as a challenge and guide. They are human and Christian qualities which will grow in catechists as they exercise their ministry (205).

Catechists are meant to be witnesses to the Gospel, faithful persons fully committed to Christ. The faith of catechists ought to be so strong and so central in their lives that they are compelled to share it with conviction, joy, love and enthusiasm. This faith is not static, but like all living relationships is always changing, growing stronger or weakening. So that it may grow stronger catechists should be men and women of prayer. They should be persons who desire to express their faith in building community and in service (207).

Catechists are people who are committed to the

Church. They recognize that the Church as a pilgrim people is in constant need of renewal (208). Realizing that this visible and imperfect community is called to deeper holiness, they strive to help it be more faithful to its calling by doing what they can to build it up through prayer, through service, and by proclaiming Christ's message to it.

Catechists are persons who have learned the meaning of community by experiencing it. They share in the life of the Church, in the Eucharist, in its service, in its mission to the world (209).

Catechists recognize that they are servants of the community. They seek out and respond to the needs of individuals and communities and encourage others to do so also. They are committed to serving whenever and wherever they can. They are sensitive to the many complex problems of injustice in our society and within the community of nations and do what they can to bring about peace and justice (210).

These "ideal qualities" of catechists are those qualities which all committed Christians are challenged to express in their lives. They describe what the Christian community is called to be. Throughout the ages men and women in all parts of the world have responded to this challenge. Many Catholic men and women in the United States have so responded. Today they continue to offer to go forth and build up the community, proclaim the message, lead others to worship, and motivate to service. The directory was written to challenge, support and encourage all catechists to share with the community the light of their faith.

Study Questions for "The Catechist"

1. What is the fundamental task of the catechist?

2. Why is it important to recognize the limits of what catechists can do? Do you feel some catechists get very discouraged because they try to do the impossible? Explain.

3. Who are the primary catechists of children? Do you think most parents see themselves in the role of catechist? How can they be helped to see their important role?

4. Why is it important for a parish catechist to see her/his role in a community context? How can the consciousness of the whole community be raised to a greater understanding of its role in catechizing?

5. Of the competencies listed in this chapter from the directory, with which do you feel most comfortable? With which do you feel most inadequate? Are there opportunities available in your local area to heighten your competency in areas in which you feel inadequate? To whom can you raise such questions? Remember, no one can be expected to be competent in all the areas listed. But the community should be able to provide expertise in the designated areas.

6. What is the responsibility of diocesan leaders

to provide for adequate training for the catechetical community? How is this expedited in your diocese?

7. What do you see as the major value of a rich community experience? If one of the major catechetical goals is to form community, it seems that the catechists should have rich community experiences out of which to operate. Brainstorm about how this can be done in your parish or school.

Articles in the NCD that refer to the catechist						
Preface	Chapter 1	Chapter 2	Chapter 3	Chapter 4	Chapter 5	Chapter 6
6	16	47	60	74		134
9	29			79		139
						140
						141
						142
						145
						146
						147

	Chapter 7	Chapter 8	Chapter 9	Chapter 10	Chapter 11
	166	175	All	221	249
	170	176	of	222	252
		179	this	223	253
		180	Chapter	226	256
		181		227	258
		185		228	259
		187		229	260
		190		232	261
		191		237	265
		194			
		197			
		200			
		203			